THE WRATH OF GRAPES

THE
WRATH of GRAPES

DRINKING
AND
THE CHURCH DIVIDED

ANDRE S. BUSTANOBY

BAKER BOOK HOUSE
Grand Rapids, Michigan 49516

Contents

Preface

The Grape that can with Logic absolute
The Two-and-Seventy jarring Sects confute:
The subtle Alchemist that in a trice
Life's leaden Metal into Gold transmute.
The Rubáiyát of Omar Khayyám

Wine lovers will agree with this poetic sentiment. Indeed, they will join Omar Khayyám in praise of the alchemist's magic. Legalistic prohibitionists will, however, denigrate the transmutation with equal vigor. But both will agree that the grape does indeed "the Two-and-Seventy jarring Sects confute."

This book is not intended to jar but rather to offer a reasoned defense of Christian liberty as it applies to alcohol use. But it is more. It is a warning that this transmuted gold may turn out to be fool's gold. Though the Bible permits alcohol *use*, it warns against its *abuse*.

There is no lack of documentation regarding the damage inflicted on individuals and society by those who use alcohol to excess, despite the media's rosy characterization of wine, beer, and distilled spirits as an "innocent" pleasure, a personal relaxant and easy route to social camaraderie. Medical professionals attest to the potential harm effected by alcohol on the mind and body of the excessive drinker. Furthermore, neither abstainers nor those who drink "sensibly" can afford to ignore the consequences suffered by an abuser's loved ones. Beyond the individual case histories of fragmented lives and lost potential, society at large pays an untold price when alcohol is used immoderately by its members. Newspaper headlines and alarming statistics underscore the injuries and deaths caused by drunk drivers and the significant percentage of crimes directly related to alcohol abuse.

It is both sound theology and practical psychology to state that— whether alcohol is used in moderation or to excess—the drinker himself must be held responsible for his choice to drink. (Throughout this book I will use the masculine pronoun to refer to "the drinker." This is merely a semantic device, however, since it goes without saying that the alcohol user might be either male or female. In fact, there is increasing evidence to support the belief that more women are using—and abusing—alcohol than ever before.)

The purpose of this book is twofold. First, it presents reasons, backed by Scripture, to uphold the thesis that the choice to use alcohol is allowable within the Christian ethic. The important corollary to this position, of course, is that the user is accountable for his choice to drink, in that his actions affect others and himself. And, as with any human behavior that is "legal" in the eyes of God (and the state), excess is to be avoided. Second, I will provide suggestions for those whose lives have been disrupted and damaged by an alcohol abuser or alcoholic in their midst. Family members and close associates will be given specific instructions about what they must do to place accountability for abuse where it belongs—on the shoulders of the abuser.

Libertarians must not be blind to the problem of alcohol abuse, though the solution is not in legalistic prohibition by church bodies or government. It lies in the intelligent use of liberty.

Andre Bustanoby
Lancaster, Virginia

1

Liberty or Legalism?

They looked like a contented, solid couple—about sixty-five years old. I ate my supper as I watched them waiting for the hostess to seat them. They finally took the restaurant table next to mine.

His hair was Friar Tuck style—bald on the top, with remnants surviving on the sides and back and badly in need of trimming. He wore a white polyester short-sleeved dress shirt and tie with slacks and wingtip shoes.

She amply filled her turquoise polyester pantsuit. They were no fashion plates, but they looked like a happy couple.

Before they started munching on the crackers and cheese in front of them, they joined hands and said grace. *What a sweet picture*, I thought. It was a living Norman Rockwell portrait. Not just a solid American couple but a solid American *Christian* couple.

Their waitress arrived and asked if they would like something from the bar. Imagine my surprise when the woman looked up with her chubby face beaming and said, "Yes. I'd like a glass of burgundy wine." Her husband told the waitress to give him a glass, too.

But why was I so surprised? This was not the Bible Belt. I had forgotten that I was in Grand Rapids, Michigan—not only geographically distant from Birmingham or Fort Worth, but culturally far removed as well. This was a city steeped in Old World tradition where the Christians had a far different view of drinking. Though a Bible Belt believer would not be seen doing it, this couple saw no contradiction in saying grace and then ordering a glass of wine.

But what I perceived that evening as merely an interesting regional difference between Christians, others feel is a scourge to the church. To many, the idea of Christians drinking alcoholic beverages is positively scandalous.

The book *Sipping Saints* is a good example. Author David Wilkerson says,

> I seriously doubt Christians who drink can be called saints. I call them "sipping saints," only because they are self-confessed Christians who drink. . . . I cannot understand how a Spirit-filled Christian, who confesses that his tongue has been sanctified and yielded to God for the use of heavenly languages, can turn around and pickle that same tongue with alcohol.[1]

The book goes on to declare how wrong it is for Christians to drink any amount of alcohol and takes issue with all who say otherwise.

The grape does indeed the two- and seventy jarring sects confute!

But division in the church over eating and drinking is not something new. Since the first century, sincere Christians have argued over what is proper for a Christian to consume. For example, in New Testament times Christians argued over eating meat from idolatrous sacrifices. The advocates of liberty maintained that such meat was fit to eat, while the legalists decried the practice as sin.

The apostle Paul, addressing this general problem, maintained that whatever God does not declare sinful is lawful (1 Cor. 10:23). Christians applying this principle to alcohol use today say that though drunkenness is sin, drinking is not—an assertion to be proved in the forthcoming chapters.

But the advocates of Christian liberty are not primarily interested in the right to drink. They are concerned with the larger issue of

---

1. David Wilkerson, *Sipping Saints*, back cover.

legalism, which denies the Christian the right to do *anything* the legalist believes to be sin.

God gives every believer the freedom to do anything the Bible does not declare sinful. And this includes drinking—though the believer may choose not to exercise that right. But it is *his* choice. That right of individual choice is at the heart of the liberty/legalism debate.

In order to understand this, we must first understand something about legalism both historically and in its modern expression.

Legalism in Jesus' Day

The religious laws of Israel, which God delivered to Moses, governed both religious and secular life. But the rabbis felt that the people needed to have the law interpreted for them so they would know how it was to be applied in cases not made clear by Scripture.

As a result, there emerged a body of writings known as the Talmud, which the rabbis considered as authoritative as Scripture. They justified their high view of the Talmud on the ground that Scripture *implied* all the laws the Talmud made explicit. The Talmud, therefore, carried authority equal to that of Scripture.[2] By imposing the Talmud on the people, the rabbis became "legalists." They made their interpretation of the law equal in authority to the God-given law. They themselves were lawmakers.

But these implied rules of behavior were an impossible burden to the people. What is more, the religious establishment was of no help in aiding the people with this impossible demand (Luke 11:46). It was in this context that Jesus offered his followers something different: a yoke that is easy and a burden that is light (Matt. 11:30).

In order to keep track of and teach the people the many regulations of the Talmud, the rabbis trained ecclesiastical lawyers to do the job. These religious lawyers became the aristocrats of Israel. Such a lawyer, also known as a Scribe, was the authority on all matters religious and had the absolute respect of the people. He was regarded "a well-plastered pit, filled with the water of knowledge, out of which not one

---

2. Alfred Edersheim, *The Life and Times of Jesus the Messiah*, vol. 1, p. 100.

drop can escape."[3] He stood above the simple, ignorant country people who did not know the law. In this position the lawyers were a proud lot and religiously arrogant. By enforcing the Talmud as equally binding as Scripture, they too became legalists, as are all those who make and enforce laws that go beyond what Scripture teaches.

It is no wonder, then, that this religious elite clashed with Jesus, who offered the people *himself* rather than the law. He offered gentleness and humility in exchange for spiritual pride and arrogance. He offered a burden that was light in exchange for a burden impossible to carry. In his substitutionary death on the cross, Jesus would in one moment of time do away with the scrupulous observance of legalistic doctrine as a way of relating to God. He would introduce liberty as the way of life—liberty to do whatever the Bible itself does not declare sin.

Legalism in the New Testament Church

The practice of legalism did not die with the advent of Christ. It dogged and divided the New Testament church. Jews raised in the old system, which revered both the Bible and the Talmud, carried over their legalism into Christianity when they accepted Jesus as their Messiah. Immediately this brought them into conflict with the Gentile Christians who were not bound by the same traditions and scruples.

Legalism in Rome. Two traditions that became a source of friction in the early church were the Jewish Christians' observance of certain holy days and their avoidance of any food that might have been "tainted" by the Gentiles. What they ate was strictly dictated by the Jewish dietary code. They ate only "kosher" food—that which is "right" or "fit," according to those ancient laws.

The friction was due to the spiritual pride and arrogance of the Jewish Christians, who regarded themselves as more spiritual than the Gentile Christians who did not adhere to the observance of holy days and ate "unclean" food.

---

3. Ibid., p. 93.

The apostle Paul wrote about this problem in Romans 14 and 15. His judgment was that those who must impose rules upon themselves beyond what the Scripture imposes are actually "weak" Christians (Rom. 14:1–2). However, if a person, because of his rearing, imposes these restrictions upon himself so he might not *feel* guilty, that is permissible (Rom. 14:5–6). At the same time, he must not impose these restrictions on others or judge them for not doing what he does.

Likewise, the Christian who enjoys his liberty must not judge those who feel they must restrict their own freedom. Christian liberty allows us to do whatever the Bible does not declare sinful (Rom. 14:13–21), but we are to respect the scruples of those who do not choose to exercise that liberty. Though *we* do not feel bound, we are to respect the fact that *they* do.

Legalism in Corinth. The same truth is taught in 1 Corinthians 8–11. Gentile Christians are warned not to permit their exercise of liberty to become a cause for the weaker brother to trip over that example and fall into sin (1 Cor. 8:9–13). Though everything not declared sinful in the Scripture is permissible or lawful, everything is not beneficial—either for the person who feels free to exercise liberty or for those who observe him exercising that prerogative. Liberty is not a careless right. It is to be exercised with caution (1 Cor. 10:23–11:1).

The apostle Paul makes it clear that abstinence and the restriction of liberty are permitted so long as these acts are recognized as a *weakness* rather than spiritual strength and that the one who abstains does not regard himself spiritually superior to or more knowledgeable than those who do not abstain. Paul would have no "Talmud" in the New Testament church. If the Jewish Christians needed to exercise their scruples as a personal matter, that was their choice. But their scruples were not to be added to the list of sins already stated in Scripture.

Legalism in Colossae. In spite of Paul's teachings on legalism in his letters to the Romans and Corinthians, legalism hung on in the church and became a monstrous problem in Colossae. In fact, it was so destructive to Christian faith and practice that Paul launched his most vigorous attack on it in his letter to the Colossians.

The error in Colossae was legalism mixed with an asceticism that viewed the material world as intrinsically evil and thus to be avoided. To these legalists one's spirituality was shown by strict observance of dietary rules and holy days (Col. 2:16). As true legalists, they even forbade practices that the Scripture does not forbid. They drank no wine and ate no animal food. They were strict vegetarians. They condemned the gratification of all natural cravings as "worldly," and women were regarded as mere instruments of temptation—deceitful, faithless, selfish, jealous, misled and misleading by their passions.[4] These legalists felt bound to add their scruples—their traditional restrictions—to Scripture itself. They taught these principles as though they carried the authority of Scripture. They had to have their Talmud! They could not handle Christian liberty.

In spite of their abhorrence of sin, their legalistic behavior actually prompted sin, by engendering a false humility that resulted in spiritual pride (Col. 2:18). They were so "humble" that they did not believe they deserved to talk directly to God, so they appealed to angels to mediate their prayers.[5] But they took great pride in their humility! This pride was manifested in their belief that they lived spiritual lives superior to all other Christians—lives based on a purportedly superior knowledge of spiritual things. Paul says, "Don't let this kind of person dominate you and prescribe what you should do or not do to win your heavenly reward. He'll mislead you and actually get you disqualified from receiving a prize" (Col. 2:18, paraphrased).

Not only were these people prideful, they were also guilty of unbiblical asceticism with their "Do not handle! Do not taste! Do not touch!" (Col. 2:21). These restrictions included abstinence from wine, meat, and even wholesome relations with the opposite sex. Paul had some harsh words for these people. He accused them of engaging in self-imposed worship of angels, who were supposed to mediate the prayers of humans too humble to go directly to God. But this was a false humility. He also accused them of treating their bodies harshly by their ascetic practices. Paul acknowledged that these things might

4. J. B. Lightfoot, *Saint Paul's Epistles to the Colossians and to Philemon*, pp. 85–87.
5. John Albert Bengel, *Gnomon of the New Testament*, p. 176.

appear, to the new Christian, as wise things to do. But the reality is that "they lack any value in restraining sensual indulgence" (Col. 2:23). This is a bold statement and sure to rile the legalist. He will say, "Just look at the lives of those whom you call legalists and tell me that their strict views of separation from the world don't work. No Christian who lives a separated Christian life and hates worldliness will ever have a problem with alcohol!"

I must agree that if a person stays in bondage to legalism all of his life, he will most likely avoid alcohol abuse. Legalistic churches are subcultures in this regard, much like ethnic groups that treat drunkenness as taboo and have strong social sanctions against it. A person need not be a legalist to be a teetotaler. He just needs to be part of a strong culture that treats drunkenness as absolutely forbidden.

But this person faces a big problem as soon as he discovers that legalism runs contrary to biblical teachings and repudiates it. He is then in double jeopardy. Not only does he give up the safety of the culture whose taboos protected him against such gross misconduct as drunkenness, but his disillusionment also encourages rebellion and an "I'll show you" attitude that may lead to a life of indulgence. The backlash reaction to legalism can easily lead to an evil just as bad—license!

In espousing the doctrine of liberty, I am well aware of the danger of license. But license—the self-indulgent repudiation of legalism— is as much a denial of liberty as legalism. Liberty teaches us that whatever is not sinful is lawful. But not everything that is lawful is the smart thing to do! License denies that it may be the wiser course not to indulge ourselves.

What Paul is saying in Colossians 2:23 may be paraphrased this way:

> Such regulations [that the legalists invent] do have an appearance of wisdom with their self-imposed [not divinely imposed] restrictions, but it results in false humility and harsh treatment of the body. This is not God's way of restraining sensual indulgence.

Historical legalism offers an unbiblical substitute for God's way of restraining sin under grace. God's way is to place on us the responsibility to decide what may not be a smart thing to do. It places on us the responsibility to set our own limits on practices that may be perfectly lawful.

Modern Legalism

Today's religious legalism does exactly what its historical counterpart did. It undermines Christian liberty in a number of ways:

1. It elevates the legalistic interpretation of Scripture to a tradition that is equal in authority to Scripture itself. For example, the Scripture says that drunkenness is a sin. The legalist declares that since drinking can lead to drunkenness, drinking is therefore sinful. In effect, legalistic writings on the subject of the spiritual life become a new Talmud. The words *legalist* and *legalism* come from this practice. The religious legalist is a person who adds to the laws or prohibitions already stated in Scripture and attempts to use these laws as a way of holding down sin in the lives of all Christians.

2. It burdens believers with so many restrictions that the Christian life continually focuses on what we ought not to do rather than what we can do with our freedom and liberty in Christ. It ignores the fact that Christ's yoke is easy and his burden is light. It takes the joy out of being a Christian.

3. It teaches that self-imposed restrictions are a sign of spiritual strength, whereas Scripture makes it clear that it is an evidence of weakness.

4. It teaches that a legalistically restrictive lifestyle results in a spirituality superior to those whose lifestyle is less restrictive. But those who promote this idea are as guilty of puffed-up spiritual pride as were the Colossians. And they are spiritually the worse for it.

5. It is unbiblical in its doctrine of the spiritual life because it denies the truth of Christian liberty under grace, as taught in Romans 14–15, 1 Corinthians 8–11, and Colossians 2:16–23.

6. It promotes unbiblical asceticism. Ascetics demand that the appetites of the body be denied simply because natural cravings are supposed to be wrong. Ascetics always set natural or bodily cravings against what they regard as spiritual cravings. The ascetic legalist teaches that spiritual cravings are the only cravings we should have. He calls "impure" what "God has made clean" (Acts 10:15).

The ascetic element of legalism can be heard in the hymnology of its churches. One of the old favorites goes:

> Oh, how the thought of God attracts
> And draws the heart from earth,
> And sickens it of passing shows
> And dissipating mirth!
>
> 'Tis not enough to save our souls
> To shun the eternal fires;
> The thought of God will rouse the heart
> To more sublime desires.
>
> God only is the creature's home
> Though rough and straight the road;
> Yet nothing less can satisfy
> To love that longs for God.[6]

The idea that God's creation is "sickening" and "dissipating" when compared to God is unbiblical. We must not call unclean what God calls clean.

Another hymnwriter, speaking for God, says,

> Am I not enough, Mine own? enough,
>   Mine own, for thee?
> Hath the world its palace towers,
> Garden glades of magic flowers,
>   Where thou fain wouldst be?
>
> Fair things and false are there,
> False things but fair.
> All shalt thou find at last,
>   Only in Me.
>
> Am I not enough, Mine own? I, for ever
>   and alone, I, needing thee?[7]

How can God, who called his creation good, declare that the palace towers and garden glades of magic flowers are "false"? How can God,

---

6. C. Holden, *The Christian Book of Mystical Verse*, ed. A. W. Tozer, pp. 51–52.
7. Ibid., p. 111.

who said, "It is not good for man to be alone," say in this hymn, "Am I not enough"? No, he is not! God made us social creatures with a need for each other, not for himself alone!

Though most legalists are sincere people who want to promote godliness, legalism is not the way to do it. The denial of proper and lawful appetites, whether for companionship, food, or drink, runs contrary to the biblical doctrine of Christian liberty.

Legalists, though well intentioned, are also dangerous. Just like the Scribes in Jesus' day, they bend Scripture to conform to their own traditions and prejudices, which fundamentally are ascetic. But we will let them speak for themselves in the next chapter.

2

Legalistic Objections

In December 1976 Billy Graham, responding favorably to President Carter's decision not to serve anything stronger than wine in the White House, said in an interview, "I do not believe that the Bible teaches teetotalism . . . . Jesus drank wine. Jesus turned water into wine at a wedding feast. That wasn't grape juice as some try to claim."[1]

This statement provoked an anguished outcry from legalistic prohibitionists, so Graham responded by issuing another one in which he came down hard on the evils of alcohol and encouraged total abstinence as a practical matter. Said Graham,

> It is my judgment that because of the devastating problem that alcohol has become in America, it is better for Christians to be teetotalers except for medicinal purposes. . . . The creeping paralysis of alcoholism is sapping our morals, wrecking our homes, and luring people away from the church.[2]

---

1. "Carter Will Restore Confidence, Graham Says," *Miami Herald*, 26 December 1976: sec. A, 18.
2. "Graham On Drink: 'Don't,'" *Christianity Today* (February 4, 1977): 63.

But legalists are not satisfied with this approach to alcohol either. They are convinced that alcoholic beverages are "innately sinful."[3] But let's hear their side of the story. . . .

Criticism of the Alcohol User

The legalist offers four criticisms of the alcohol user. Though wine is the primary focus of their criticism, mainly because it is the most frequently mentioned beverage in the Bible, the legalist's objections apply to all alcoholic beverages.

"The alcohol user is inconsistent." The legalist says that the alcohol user who abstains only out of love for the weaker brother is inconsistent. He argues that if God creates something good for man, why should it be set aside because it is not accepted by the "weaker brethren"? Indeed, if wine *is* a good gift from God, should not the weaker brethren be so informed and be taught to use it?

The legalist draws an analogy from sexual relationships. He agrees that sex is a God-created gift to be enjoyed in marriage. But let us suppose, he says, that a biblically ignorant Christian, offended at the high incidence of sex outside of marriage, should develop a low view of sex altogether—even in marriage. Married Christians do not refrain from sex because of a weaker brother's objections. In this case, he is an uninformed Christian and needs to be informed about the rightness of sex in marriage.[4]

This illustration is not farfetched, and this was one of the problems at Colossae with the legalists. They discouraged wholesome sexual relations. But the answer to this objection is very simple. The Bible leaves no doubt about the issue of sex. It is absolutely clear that sex within the bonds of marriage is a positive good. Outside of marriage it is a sin. Therefore, sexually abstinent married persons need help in

---

3. This is the position taken by Robert P. Teachout in his Th.D. dissertation, "The Use of 'Wine' in the Old Testament" (Dallas: Dallas Theological Seminary, 1982), p. 330. This position is also taken by David Wilkerson in *Sipping Saints* and Dr. Jack Van Impe in *Alcohol: The Beloved Enemy*.

4. Teachout, "The Use of 'Wine,'" pp. 314–15.

seeing their error, and the married who are sexually active need not abstain from sex within the marital relationship.

But the issue of alcohol use is not that clear in Scripture. In fact, the legalistic prohibitionist readily admits that most lexicons and commentaries support the contention that fermented beverages were used by believers in Bible times. With few exceptions, the most conclusive statement the legalist can make about the words for "wine" in the Bible is that a particular word *could* mean unfermented grape juice, or it is *possibly* unfermented, or it is *assumed* to be unfermented—or there is a lack of agreement among scholars.[5]

Because this is an interpretive issue and fraught with disagreement, we dare not dogmatize on the use of alcohol. But we *can* dogmatize about alcohol *abuse*. It is sin. But alcohol use itself is a debatable or "disputable" matter, subject to the law of liberty (Rom. 14:1).

For this very reason, we ought not encourage the abstainer to use alcohol. Such an act would be insensitive to his scruples and a clear violation of Romans 14:1, which says, "Accept him whose faith is weak, without passing judgment on disputable matters." Since this matter *is* disputable, the abstainer's scruples are to be respected.

There is no shame in saying, "I can't drink. I'm too weak." For some the weakness arises from a rearing that makes drinking an unthinkable violation of conscience. Others, such as I, are weak because our personalities are so constituted as to abuse alcohol.[6] The candid admission of weakness goes a long way to keep us from pride and the evil of being coerced into exercising a liberty we cannot handle. Others may drink; we cannot.

"Most alcohol users don't know Hebrew and Greek." The legalist argues, in the second place, that the language of Bible lexicons (Hebrew and Greek dictionaries) and Bible translations where "wine" is apparently approved of leads people to accept the use of wine without further inquiry.[7] He maintains that the words translated "wine" *could* mean "grape juice." So he says that without further study,

---

5. Ibid., pp. 115–17, 119, 125, 127, 135, 138–39, 148, 151, 155.
6. "Genes, Personality and Alcoholism," *Psychology Today* (January 1985): 38.
7. Teachout, "The Use of 'Wine,'" p. 317.

the average Christian naively assumes that wine, the fermented drink, was widely used by believers.

The legalist tells us that the problem is "lexical" (dealing with the meaning of words), but it is not. It is interpretive. The fact of the matter is that even a further study of the words in Hebrew and Greek offers no conclusive evidence in support of the legalist's position. It comes down to interpretation of Scripture, which, we shall see, readily lends itself to the traditional interpretation of "wine" as a fermented beverage.

"The alcohol user is naive." In the third place, the legalist maintains that users are naive if they think that the alcoholic content of wine in Bible times was low enough to provide a control on drunkenness. He says that the wine in Bible times was between 12 and 14 percent, sufficient to get a person drunk—as the Bible itself attests.[8]

This is true enough, up to a point. However, we shall see that only the best wine was fully aged and high in alcohol content. The poor, who were in the majority, had to settle for a cheap, low-alcohol beverage. And there is evidence that the diluting of wine was common not only to the Greco-Roman world of the first century, but also among the Jews centuries before.

"The alcohol user argues out of ignorance." The preservation of grape juice is another issue in the debate. The fourth point the legalistic prohibitionist tries to make is that alcohol users argue out of ignorance when they say that the ancients could not have preserved grape juice between the yearly harvest of grapes. The legalist maintains that methods of preservation were both known and used.[9]

I will take up this subject in the next two chapters, so I will not deal with the specifics here. But we shall see that the "evidences" for the preservation of grape juice that the legalistic prohibitionists offer are seriously flawed. They completely misunderstand what ancient historians have to say about winemaking because they themselves do not understand the chemistry of wine. The recipes that come down from ancient historians do not tell us how to preserve grape juice. Rather, they tell us how to make wine and keep it from turning into vinegar.

---

8. Ibid., pp. 320–21.
9. Ibid., pp. 326–29.

The Legalist Defends His Criticism

The legalist defends his criticism of the alcohol user with four arguments:

1. "Wine" in the Bible may be grape juice
2. The grape was God's best gift to his people
3. Wine is a perversion of God's gift
4. "Wine" was to be enjoyed without limit[10]

"'Wine' may be grape juice." In defending his criticism of alcohol use, the legalistic prohibitionist says, first of all, that the words used for wine in Old Testament Hebrew and languages related to Hebrew *may mean* either wine or grape juice. The italics are mine, and I make the emphasis to demonstrate the paucity of evidence for the hard line the legalist takes. I agree that the word translated "wine" in the Bible at times may sometimes mean grape juice.

But the legalist then does a neat bit of logical gymnastics. He says that since this is true, whenever the Bible speaks favorably of "wine," it is not referring to the fermented beverage but rather to grape juice. On the other hand, whenever the Bible condemns "wine," it must be referring to the fermented beverage. We shall see in the forthcoming chapters that this is nonsense.[11]

"The gift of the grape." The legalist argues, in the second place, that the gift of the grape is one of God's greatest gifts to his people, Israel. He says that the patriarchal blessings of Isaac and Jacob as well as those from God bear this out. God owned the land, and it was to be used with a sense of his blessing. Likewise, judgment against the nation's apostasy resulted in the loss of the land's fertility.[12] This argument, though true, is used to imply that the Jews, prior to their

---

10. Ibid., pp. 313–36.

11. Ibid., pp. 329–30. Teachout says that the problem is lexical (the meaning of words) rather than theological. But it is not lexical. It is interpretive, requiring a thorough understanding of the chemistry of wine and ancient man's use of that chemistry.

12. Ibid., pp. 130–31.

apostasy, did not drink fermented wine. There is no historical evidence to support this inference.

"Wine is a perversion of the gift." In the third place, according to the legalist, the grape was to be used in its unfermented state. Wine was a perversion of its intended use. The purpose of grape juice was to "rejoice the heart of man," not to make it "merry," which is the property of an intoxicant. Wine is strongly denounced in the Bible, according to the legalist, because it is a perverson of God's best gift.

We should ask, then, "Why does God go into such detail in Deuteronomy about other restrictions but neglect to instruct the people carefully on this immensely important issue?" I can only conclude that drinking wine was not a sin.

God gave the law to Israel so they would know exactly what was expected of them. The Bible is very clear in naming sin in act or principle. Therefore, the apostle Paul can be very confident in teaching us that we are free to do anything the Bible does not declare sin. *All things not sinful are lawful* (1 Cor. 10:23).

The use of alcohol is clearly a debatable matter and therefore falls under the rule of Christian liberty. Legalistic prohibitionists do the church a great disservice when they insist on imposing a new Talmud on God's people—their personal view of sin.

"'Wine' without limit." Finally, the legalists point out that several passages of the Old Testament encourage God's people to drink to their fill of the fruit of the vine (Song of Sol. 5:1). "How," they ask, "can God's people be expected to enjoy fermented wine without limit if it is intoxicating?"

There are several answers to this, all of which will be elaborated on as we get into specific Scriptures. But I should make several observations here.

First, the Book of Proverbs gives us ample warning about limits. Israel, by this time, had sufficient experience with alcohol to require the instruction given in Proverbs. And they were instructed to be moderate, not abstinent.

Second, to say that the grape was a gift to be used without limit ignores what the Book of Proverbs says about limits on both wine and food. The glutton and the drunkard are frequently mentioned together in the Bible. Why does the legalist single out the drunkard for condemnation but not condemn the glutton? Limits *were* put on God's people.

Third, there is evidence that relatively large quantities of fermented wine could be drunk because it was liberally diluted with water. This was a custom among the Jews in Old Testament times as well as among the Greeks and Romans in the first century. Wine drinking in those days was more a challenge to the bladder than to the equilibrium.

Fourth, there was an economic restraint on the use of intoxicating wine. Though God did indeed bless his people, good aged wine (three years old) was not commonly drunk. The common drink was a low-alcohol beverage made from the rinsing of the wine vat. These are some of the arguments we shall examine in the forthcoming chapters.

Finally, the most critical question of all is whether believers in Old and New Testament times preserved grape juice in an unfermented state. To say that they did shows a serious misunderstanding of the chemistry of winemaking and leads to false interpretation of historical evidences. We will next consider the chemistry of winemaking and dispel some myths about wine.

3

Dispelling Myths About Wine

The legalist, in pressing his case against fermented wine, contends that the wine consumed by believers in biblical times was not fermented wine as we know it today but grape juice. One writer says, for example, "Were the ancients in the habit of preserving and using as such, free from fermentation, the juice of the grape? Beyond all doubt they were."[1]

Yet, in spite of this bold assurance, we must seriously doubt claims about the preservation of grape juice. Legalistic prohibitionists grossly misinterpret both the Bible and ancient historians, simply because they do not understand the chemistry of winemaking. If they did, they would not make the outrageous claims they pass for fact.

It is therefore important, before we examine what the Bible has to say about wine, that we know something about its biochemistry. The same laws of chemistry that apply to winemaking today also applied to the ancients. Knowing what these principles are and how they were used will help us avoid false exegesis and some farfetched ideas about the nature of wine in biblical times.

---

1. David Wilkerson, *Sipping Saints*, p. 53.

I shall limit my remarks in this chapter to the juice of the grape because it is the principal beverage (other than water) used by Jews and Christians. Other beverages, both intoxicating and nonintoxicating, were used, and they will be discussed in due course. I also shall limit the information on winemaking to the bare essentials. Any home vintner knows that the production of good wine requires more care than I indicate here.

Crushing and Aerobic Fermentation

The grape must go through several stages before it becomes wine. The first of these involves crushing and aerobic fermentation.

The whole grape is crushed, together with skins and seeds. The juice of the grape is called "must." It is important to understand, however, that must is not just the fresh juice of the grape. The term *must* refers to both the fresh juice of the grape *and* the juice when it is at any stage of aerobic fermentation. It is incorrect to say that must is the *unfermented* juice of the grape.[2] It sometimes is unfermented, but it sometimes is aerobically fermented.

Aerobic ferment has to do with the production of life with the help of air (*aero* + *bios*). In this context, "life" is the multiplication of yeast in an environment of free oxygen, such as open air. Aerobic fermentation is distinguished from anaerobic fermentation, wherein there is life *without* free oxygen. Prior to anaerobic fermentation, even though the must is in ferment, it is not yet wine. Must becomes wine when it is subject to anaerobic fermentation. Failure to distinguish between aerobic and anaerobic fermentation has caused no end of confusion and false exegesis. The must does not technically become wine until it goes through *anaerobic* ferment, even though it previously fermented *aerobically.*

Yeast, which is found naturally everywhere, converts the sugar of the grape into alcohol. The higher the sugar content of the grape, the higher will be the alcoholic content of the finished product.

---

2. Robert Teachout, "The Use of 'Wine' in the Old Testament," p. 23.

In ancient times winemakers depended on wild yeast to aerobically ferment the must in the wine vat—ferment that began even as
they were treading out the grapes. Not understanding the chemistry
of fermentation, they were left with uncertain results. If a weak wild
yeast produced the ferment, a weak (about 4 percent alcohol) wine
resulted. If the winemakers were fortunate enough to have a hardy
wine yeast work the must, they could expect an alcohol content of 15
percent or more.[3]

The purpose of this step—aerobic fermentation—is to multiply
the yeast, which turns the sugar of the fruit into alcohol. The must is
subject to aerobic ferment for anywhere from ten days to four weeks.
The Romans allowed must to ferment for a year before bottling it for
anaerobic ferment.[4]

A lot of confusion and false exegesis has resulted from a failure to
understand this. In legalistic literature there is a lot of talk about the
use in Bible times of must, which people drank instead of wine—as
though they were not drinking a fermented beverage. But must is the
juice of the grape in aerobic ferment. Though must is not the finished
product, aged wine, they were in fact drinking a fermented beverage.

The difference between must and wine is the same as the difference between hard cider and apple wine, both of which are capable
of making a person drunk. Hard cider is the juice of the apple in the
aerobic ferment. But apple wine requires that the juice also be put
through anaerobic ferment in a sealed container.

People drink the juice of the apple at three stages of development:
as cider (unfermented), as hard cider (aerobically fermented), and as
apple wine (both aerobically and anaerobically fermented).

Grape must in aerobic ferment often goes by the name "new wine."
As we shall see, the ancients drank the juice of the grape at all states

---

3. William Younger, *Gods, Men, and Wine*, p. 25.
4. The difference is the same as in hard cider and apple wine, both of which are
capable of producing intoxication. Cider, which is very low in alcohol content, is
permitted to get "hard" by letting the yeast in it work aerobically and produce
more alcohol. But the juice must ferment *anaerobically* to produce apple wine.
People drink the juice of the apple in three stages of ferment: as cider, hard cider,
and apple wine. Refrigeration today makes possible the preservation of unfermented apple juice as well.

of its production: prior to ferment, during aerobic ferment (when it was "new wine"), and after anaerobic ferment (when it was true wine).

Pressing and Anaerobic Fermentation

The second step in the winemaking process is pressing and anaerobic fermentation. When the aerobic ferment is quiet, the must is then pressed and the juice is allowed to run off into a container. The container is then securely stoppered. Must is not stoppered to retard further fermentation, as one writer suggests.[5] It is stoppered to begin the process of anaerobic fermentation, which is the birth of the wine.[6]

Anaerobic fermentation, or fermentation without free oxygen, is a marvelous process that was not understood until modern times. To denigrate fermented wine as decay and symbolic of death shows no understanding of anaerobic fermentation—life without free oxygen.[7]

Anaerobic fermentation is found not only in ageing wine but also in the chemistry of the human body. In the absence of free oxygen (anaerobic conditions), glucose is degraded to pyruvic acid. In the human body, muscle cells then convert the pyruvic acid into lactic acid and energy. In wine, under anaerobic conditions, the yeast enzymes convert pyruvic acid to ethyl alcohol, carbon dioxide, and energy. In the human body the process is called *glycolysis*. In ageing wine it is called *anaerobic fermentation*.[8]

In winemaking, the anaerobic ferment is permitted to continue in the stoppered container. This, of course, requires an oxygen-free environment. The ancients had a difficult time ensuring such conditions, mainly because their containers were porous, and they had no adequate way to stopper the containers since corks had not yet been invented. This often resulted in the production of inferior wine simply because the anaerobic conditions were poor or the wine turned to vinegar.

---

5. Teachout, "The Use of 'Wine,'" p. 397.
6. Jan Adkins, *The Craft of Making Wine*, p. 56.
7. Wilkerson, *Sipping Saints*, p. 21.
8. Antony Wilbraham and Michael Matta, *Introduction to Organic and Biological Chemistry*, p. 437.

The major threats to wine at this stage are free oxygen, internal pressure (which could burst the vessel), and bacteria. The ubiquitous fruit or vinegar fly spoils wine by introducing bacteria, which converts the sugar into acetic acid (vinegar) instead of alcohol. Sulfur is also an important ingredient in winemaking. It is used prior to anaerobic fermentation as an antibacterial agent. The hardy wine yeast is not affected by the sulfur and will continue anaerobic fermentation. But sulfur kills the bacteria left by the vinegar fly.

The ancients had a lot of wine turn to vinegar because they did not fully understand what caused this. They were aware that sulfur helped, but they lacked scientific precision in using it. When they referred to keeping their wine sweet by using sulfur, they were talking about keeping it from turning to vinegar. They were not preserving it as grape juice!

I am convinced that one reason why alcohol abuse was not a major problem to the ancients is that truly good, high-alcohol wine was not in great supply and was thus expensive. There was a lot of poor-quality wine of low-alcohol content. And a lot of it never became true wine—it was just aerobically fermented must.

The Stirring of the Lees

The third step is "the stirring of the lees." In the northern hemisphere winemaking is done in the fall. It ferments anaerobically in a cool (55 to 70 degrees), dry, dark, quiet place. The ferment gradually slows down until all the available sugar is converted into alcohol. Some time after the first of the year the vintner will "stir the lees." Lees are the sediment at the bottom of the vessel. The stirring is done to activate any latent ferment.

The ancient Greeks discovered quite by accident that a sea voyage aged wine much more quickly than it aged in the wine cellar.[9] The reason, of course, is that the lees were automatically stirred by the movement of the waves, activating the latent ferment. We should

---

9. Younger, *Gods, Men, and Wine*, p. 208.

remember this when we get to our discussion of Scriptures that speak of "wine on the lees."

Racking and Topping Off

The fourth step is "racking and topping off." Racking is the process of separating the clear wine from its lees. The easiest and best way to do this is to let the wine stand undisturbed so it will "throw" its lees— let the sediment sink to the bottom of the vessel. The clear or clarified wine is then siphoned off into a clean vessel.

This procedure was known by the ancients. Many engravings show wine being siphoned or drunk directly from the container through strawlike tubes. Grape wine on the lees, clarified and racked, was the most valued of all the wines and brought a high price.[10]

Wine that is to be kept for further ageing is traditionally racked and bottled after it is about a year old. The space left by the absence of the lees is filled by "topping off" with more clarified wine. The air space in the container must be kept to a minimum to maintain the anaerobic conditions.

Though the finished product takes time and care, it should be remembered that the juice of the grape in ancient times was drunk at all stages of development: fresh and unfermented; as must going through aerobic fermentation; and as anaerobically fermented wine, both young and old. Much of the confusion over the drinking habits of the ancients arises from a failure to understand this fact. Until the juice of the grape undergoes *anaerobic* fermentation, it is really not wine. It is merely fermented must or new wine of low-alcohol content.

With this information in mind, we are now ready to consider arguments of the legalist who maintains that the ancients did not drink fermented wine, but instead drank preserved grape juice.

---

10. Ibid., p. 62.

4

"Grape Juice" and Other Myths

T here is something about the grape that addles the brain and makes men say outrageous things—and this is not always due to intoxication. Both alcohol users and teetotalers are afflicted with a strange fascination for "the fruit of the vine"—a fascination that precipitates outrageous claims for and against it.

The Folklore of Winemakers and Teetotalers

Winemakers from time immemorial have had their folklore, which when seen in the light of modern chemistry is revealed for what it is— just so much unsubstantiated legend. Even in our scientifically en- lightened age, wine aficionados tell us that they can make wine out of almost anything. Books have been published offering "recipes" for grass wine, pencil-shaving wine, soap-chip wine, and goat-hair wine. While it is possible to set the forces of ferment to work on almost any organic substance, these recipes are full of overstatement, inaccuracy, and a sizable dose of folklore.[1]

---

1. Jan Adkins, *The Craft of Making Wine*, p. 75.

Teetotalers spread their share of folklore too. One prohibitionist quotes a preposterous claim by Josephus, the first-century Jewish historian, in support of his contention that the ancients knew how to preserve grape juice unfermented. Though this prohibitionist admits that Josephus' claim may *seem* preposterous, he nevertheless introduces it as "evidence."

According to Josephus, the food supplies at the Jewish fortress Masada were extraordinary:

> . . . here was laid up corn in large quantities, and such as would subsist men for a long time; here was also dates heaped up together; all which Eleazar found there, when he and his *Sicarii* got possession of the fortress by treachery. These fruits were also fresh and full ripe, and no way inferior to such fruits newly laid in, although they were little short of a hundred years from the laying in [of] these provisions [by Herod], till the place was taken by the Romans; nay, indeed when the Romans got possession of those fruits that were left, they found them not corrupted all that while: nor should we be mistaken if we supposed that the air was here the cause of their enduring so long, this fortress being so high . . . .[2]

The writer who quotes Josephus says that the report merits consideration on the ground that other ancient witnesses testify to the preservation of grape juice without fermentation.[3] But we shall see that the testimony of other ancient witnesses has to do with the process of making young, low-alcohol wine, not the preservation of grape juice. Josephus' claim is, indeed, outrageous!

But legalistic writers insist on claiming that the ancients had methods of preserving grape juice. Cato's recipe (second century B.C.) is cited as an example:

> If you wish to keep grape juice [must] through the whole year, put the grape juice [must] in an amphora, seal the stopper with pitch, and

---

2. Robert Teachout, "The Use of 'Wine' in the Old Testament," pp. 396–97.
3. Ibid.

sink in the pond. Take it out after thirty days; it will remain sweet the whole year.[4]

Cato uses the term "must," not "grape juice," in his original recipe. He is not giving us a recipe for keeping grape juice fresh. He is telling us how to keep aerobically fermented must from turning into vinegar, a problem that dogged vintners down to the nineteenth century. Keeping the must "sweet" means keeping it from turning into vinegar. This is not a recipe for preserving grape juice in an unfermented state.

Unless grape juice is kept free of yeast or bacteria, it will turn into either alcohol or vinegar. By putting the vessel "in a pond," Cato created the perfect anaerobic condition. As the must, which naturally contained yeast, fermented anaerobically, it produced alcohol and carbon dioxide. The carbon dioxide would displace any oxygen trapped in the top of the vessel and, as the pressure built, flaws in the stopper would allow the excess carbon dioxide and free oxygen to escape. In thirty days one would have a "young wine."

The same kind of low-alcohol wine is described by Pliny (second century A.D.) when he says:

> Between the sirops and real wine is the liquor that the Greeks call *aigleukos*—this is our "permanent must [semper mustum]." Care is needed for its production, as it must not be allowed to "boil [fervere]"—that is the word they use to denote the passage of must into wine. Consequently, as soon as the must is taken from the vat and put into casks, they plunge the casks in water till midwinter passes and regular cold weather sets in.[5]

We should remember that even though the juice was taken from the vat immediately and anaerobic fermentation was kept to a minimum, yeast and bacteria still contaminated the must. Again, by keeping the casks in water, anaerobic conditions were guaranteed, and the must, with a limited amount of yeast to work with, would produce a beverage of such low alcohol content, that it hardly deserved to be called wine.

---

4. Ibid., p. 397.
5. Ibid., p. 398.

Though the juice was subject to anaerobic fermentation, here it is called "permanent *must*," rather than wine. "Wine" requires both aerobic and anaerobic fermentation. But at the same time it could not be called "sirops," or grape juice, because neither aerobic nor anaerobic fermentation could be completely avoided. "Permanent must" was, therefore, a fermented drink of low-alcohol content.

Pliny's statement reinforces what I have been saying all along: the juice of the grape was drunk at all stages of production. It was drunk as grape juice ("sirops"), as low-alcohol must, and as fully aged wine.

One final word of testimony comes from Columella (first century A.D.):

> That must may remain always as sweet as though it were fresh, do as follows. Before the grape-skins are put under the press, take from the vat some of the freshest possible must and put it in a new wine-jar; then daub over and cover it carefully with pitch, that thus no water may be able to get in. Then sink the whole flagon in a pool of cold, fresh water so that no part of it is above the surface. Then after forty days take it out of the water. The must will then keep sweet for as much as a year.[6]

Columella is referring to the same process described by Cato and Pliny. Keeping the must "as sweet as though it were fresh" is somewhat of an overstatement, as vintners are prone to make. But a young, sweet, low-alcohol wine sure beats vinegar!

One final observation should be made. Even if the Greeks and Romans did use this process, Italy was a water-rich country. In Palestine there were no convenient ponds. Palestine simply didn't have enough water to make wine processed this way available to the entire nation.

Other Myths: Sulfuring, Boiling, Filtering, and Reconstituting

The legalistic prohibitionist does not limit his argument to the "evidence" given above. He maintains that the ancients had four

---

6. Ibid.

methods of preserving grape juice: sulfuring, boiling, filtering, and reconstituting the juice of dried fruit.

Sulfuring

In the previous chapter we noted the importance of sulfur in wine manufacture. It was used by the ancients to sterilize containers. Though they did not understand the chemical process, the wine-makers did use sulfur to hold down the growth of wild yeast, promote fermentation by hardy wine yeast, and discourage the vinegar fly. Instead of sulfur *preventing* fermentation, as the legalist alleges, sulfur actually aided the process of making good wine and keeping it from turning to vinegar.[7]

One reference to sulfuring that may have caused a lot of confusion among prohibitionist writers of the nineteenth century is the use of "stum" in the seventeenth century. It is not clear exactly what stum is. But some historians believe that it is "must which, by means of sulphur, had been prevented from fermenting or had been allowed only partial ferment."[8] But stum wine was not intended for drinking. The amount of raw sulfur required to prevent fermentation would have exceeded the lethal dose for human beings, to say nothing of its rotten taste.[9]

What, then, was stum wine good for? It was used to improve poor wine: "A little Stum put into Wine decayed, makes it ferment afresh and gives life and sweetness thereto. . . ."[10] The high sugar content of the stum gave the yeast in the poor wine new raw materials to work on. And the sulfur would ensure that only the hardy wine yeast would survive. This would produce a very powerful wine, much like the wine we are cautioned about in Proverbs 23:31. It is no wonder, then, that a warning went with it: "[the renewed wine] offends the head and stomach, torments the guts, and is apt to cause looseness [diarrhea?] and some say barrenness in women.[11]

7. David Wilkerson, *Sipping Saints*, pp. 32, 53.
8. William Younger, *Gods, Men, and Wine*, p. 311.
9. Ibid.
10. Ibid.
11. Ibid.

In answer, then, to the allegation that the ancients used sulfur to preserve grape juice, I agree. *But it was not used as a beverage, which could have been lethal.* It was used to give life to poor wine.

Boiling

Another alleged method of preserving grape juice is boiling. The grape juice was thereby reduced to a thick syrup, which was not supposed to ferment. It is true that a high concentration of sugar can actually destroy yeast culture.[12] But it is still subject to yeast contamination and fermentation when cooled and exposed to the air.

The custom of boiling grape juice (and fermented wine) must not be thought of as evidence of teetotalism in the ancient world. The ancients used it, as they did stum, to improve poor wine. The high sugar content gave the yeast in the poor wine new raw materials to work with.

Boiled grape juice also provided for variety in the diet of the ancients. In Egypt, about the fifteenth century B.C., the upper classes regarded fermented grape wine as the crowning glory of feasts.[13] But they also enjoyed other drinks such as beer, date wine, palm wine, and pomegranate wine. They also imbibed a drink of boiled-down grape juice or must. When further reduced it was eaten as a sweet.[14]

It is alleged by one writer that boiled wine kept unfermented forever.[15] Columella, the first-century historian, is quoted as the source of this information.

But it is no wonder that his concoction did not spoil or ferment. Columella's recipe called for the potherbs iris, fenugreek, and sweet-rush. After this herbalized must was boiled down, preservatives were added in the form of liquid pitch and turpentine resin. After this was stirred in, spices were added: the leaf of spikenard, the Illyrian sword-lily, the Gallic spikenard, the *costus*, the date, the angular rush, and the sweet-rush. Also added were myrrh, a pound of sweet reed, half a

12. Adkins, *The Craft of Making Wine*, p. 34.
13. Ibid., p. 51.
14. Ibid.
15. Teachout, "The Use of 'Wine,'" p. 399.

pound of cinnamon, balsam, saffron, and a pound of vine-leafed *cripa*. A crude pitch was mixed in with the pounded spices.[16]

I have no doubt that this substance lasted forever! No force in nature would dare assail such a concoction!

It is in this context that Columella tells us what he and his colleagues consider really good wine. The best wine is not the boiled concoction he describes or anything with preservatives. He says:

> We regard as the best wine any kind which can keep without any preservative, nor should anything be mixed with it by which its natural savor would be obscured; for that wine is most excellent which has given pleasure by its own natural qualities.[17]

The only beverage that meets these specifications is fermented wine, which keeps by the natural process of fermentation. By his own admission, Columella does not begin to compare his boiled wine with aged wine.

Filtering

Another alleged means of preservation is filtering, though it is admitted that it not easy to document conclusively.[18] Evidence is said to be given by Pliny, who reported on one occasion, "Wines are most beneficial when all their potency has been overcome by the strainer."[19]

He is referring to racking the wine and straining out the lees. The potency of the wine, as we have seen, remains in the lees and will continue to grow so long as the lees are stirred. Removing the lees would help reduce potency. But it still would be fermented wine.

Reconstituting Dried Fruit

One final means of "preserving" unfermented juice is said to be through the process of reconstituting the juice of dried fruit by soak-

16. Younger, *Gods, Men, and Wine*, p. 191.
17. Ibid.
18. Teachout, "The Use of 'Wine,'" p. 401.
19. Ibid.

ing it in water. The historian Polybius (second century B.c.) is quoted as saying:

> Among the Romans women are forbidden to drink wine; and they drink what is called *passum*, which is made from raisins, and tastes like the sweet wine (*gleukos*) of Aegosthena or Crete. This is what they do to quench their thirst. But it is almost impossible for them to drink wine without being found out.[20]

No matter how a sweet juice was produced, whether by treading the fresh grape or reconstituting its juice from the dried grape, the juice will become either wine or vinegar, given time. *Passum*, or raisin wine, could range anywhere from low to very high alcohol content, depending on when it was drunk. We saw that this was the case with the grape, which might be drunk as fresh-squeezed juice, as low-alcohol must in aerobic ferment, or as high-alcohol aged wine that had gone through anaerobic ferment.

As a matter of fact, in the colder regions of northern Italy, where the sugar content of the grape tended to be low, grapes were dried to concentrate their sugar. The raisins actually produced a fermented wine of high alcohol content![21]

Grape Juice: The Best Wine?

What did the ancients consider really *good* "wine"? And I refer not only to the Greeks and Romans but to the ancient Jews as well. According to one writer, boiled and unfermented grape juice was supposed to have been the best.[22]

Coca-Cola and Chianti. There is no question that the ancients drank a variety of beverages, both fermented and unfermented. But to say that the unfermented juice of the grape or boiled wine was considered the best wine simply is fiction. That is like comparing Coca-Cola and Chianti. Each is "the best" in its class if Coke is your preference in

---

20. Ibid., pp. 401–02.
21. Younger, *Gods, Men, and Wine*, p. 185.
22. Wilkerson, *Sipping Saints*, p. 53.

a soft drink and Chianti is your preference in wine. But they cannot be compared, because they are different types of beverages. Declaring that the unfermented juice of the grape was regarded as superior to carefully fermented and aged wine makes the same mistake. There is no comparison. Each is in a class by itself.

Columella's rave review of a "soft drink" may be one reason for this confusion. The drink is known as "after-wine." It was made of the leftovers from the manufacture of fine wine. After the first pressing of the grape, the grape "cake," or dry pulp that remained, was soaked in water. Added to the soak was the scum of boiled-down must and the dregs of the vat. After a day's soaking, the mixture was trodden, pressed, and put into jars to ferment. It produced a wine similar to the modern French *piquette*, which has about 5 percent alcohol. When Columella calls this "the best after-wine" he is not intending to compare it with good aged wine.[23]

Really good wine. What, then, was considered really good fermented grape wine? When Jesus turned water into wine at Cana (John 2), what kind of wine would the master of the banquet call "the best wine"? In Old Testament times, what did the Jews consider good wine fit for an offering to God?

1. *The Greeks and Romans.* In the first century A.D. there were eighty famous brands of wine on the Roman market, of which Italy supplied two-thirds. The finest was the Setine, the chosen drink of Augustus Caesar. The next was the Falernian, which required twenty years to mature; then the Alban, both sweet and dry, and the Massic, often mentioned by Horace. Then there was the Surrentine, which was not at its best until kept for twenty-five years, and the Mamertine, a light sweet wine, the favorite drink of Iulinus Caesar.[24]

The Romans consistently emphasized the age of their wine. One historian writes, ". . . there is no doubt whatever of the fact that matured wine was an integral part of civilized Roman life."[25] Even Columella, frequently called as a witness for the defense of the legal-

---

23. Younger, *Gods, Men, and Wine,* p. 189.
24. Harry Thurston Peck (ed.), *Harper's Dictionary of Classical Literature and Antiquities,* p. 1661.
25. Younger, *Gods, Men, and Wine,* p. 206.

istic position, says, "Almost every wine has the property of acquiring excellence with age."[26]

But the common people rarely enjoyed the truly excellent wine. Theirs was ordinary wine, drunk in the year of its vintaging.[27] The must expressed from the grape by treading was placed in large pitch-coated earthenware jars, which were placed in a wine cellar facing north to keep cool and left uncovered for a year to ferment thoroughly. Inferior wine, or must in the process of fermentation, was drunk immediately from the jar. The alcohol content would therefore vary with the degree of ferment.[28]

After its year of aerobic ferment, the better must was put in a sealed amphora (jar), closed with a stone stopper, and covered with pitch. It was labeled with information giving the year and measure. The wine was then mellowed by various means. Sometimes it was placed in the upper story of the bathhouse, where it would catch the heat and smoke of the furnace. Sometimes it was left in the sun and, as we have already seen, sometimes was sunk in water.[29]

The most famous vintage year of this period was 121 B.C. Some of this wine was still in existence in Pliny's time, about two hundred years later.[30]

One method used to improve wine in Greece and the Middle East was to keep the wine in goat skins, which allowed the evaporation of water. To produce flavor, strength, and bouquet, the Romans added gypsum, clay, chalk, marble, resin, pitch, and even seawater.[31]

The problem of adulterated wine was common, and it was often sold that way under fraudulent circumstances. This is illustrated by a graffito found at Pompeii that records the anger of a veteran gladiator at a tavern-keeper: "Curses on you, landlord, you sell water and drink unmixed wine yourself."[32]

---

26. Ibid.

27. Ibid., p. 207.

28. Peck, *Harper's Dictionary*, p. 1662.

29. Ibid.

30. Ibid.

31. Ibid.

32. Younger, *Gods, Men, and Wine*, p. 167.

Isaiah recognized this problem when he said, "Your silver has become dross / Your choice wine is diluted with water" (Isa. 1:22). Though the ancients may have diluted their wine to drink it, they didn't want to pay the full price for wine and then discover that it had been already diluted.[33]

"Good wine" to the Greeks and Romans of the first century was a fermented and well-aged product. But what of the Jews? Did *they* perhaps regard grape juice as the best "wine"?

2. *The Jews.* The Israelites of the exile and later regarded fermented, aged wine as good wine—though Jewish wine was not fermented as long as Roman wine.[34] For the most part they drank ordinary fermented wine, usually less than a year old. They appreciated "old" wine, but to them that meant year-old wine (*yayin yashan*). Very old wine was three years old (*yayin meyushan*).[35] The wines used in the temple offerings, Hattulim and Keruthin, were considered the finest quality wines, admired even by the Romans who knew good wine.[36]

The legalistic prohibitionist may reply that this is evidence of the Jews' apostasy in the exile. They not only drank fermented wine, but they also offered it in the temple! They contend that the Jews of earlier times drank grape juice, which they also supposed was offered in the temple.

The answer to this allegation is that God would not stand for an offering of "strange wine" any more than he put up with Nadab and Abihu's "unauthorized" fire (Num. 3:4). If the Jews of the exile offered the wrong wine, they would have been put to death by God.

Though fermented wine was used at this time, Israel also had its prohibitionists. For example, the Talmud, in *Sanhedrin*, says:

---

33. Antony Wilbraham and Michael Matta, *Introduction to Organic and Biological Chemistry*, p. 104. After the discovery of distillation, "proof" of alcohol content was developed for the same reason. "Proof" comes from the procedure used to test the alcoholic strength of the distilled beverage. The beverage was poured over gunpowder and a flame was touched to it. If it ignited, this was proof that the alcohol had not been watered down.

34. Younger, *Gods, Men, and Wine*, p. 75.

35. Ibid.

36. Ibid.

The Holy One, Blessed be He, said unto Noah: "Noah, should'st thou
not have taken a warning from Adam, whose transgressions was
caused by wine?" This agrees with the view that the (forbidden) tree
from which Adam ate was a vine. For it has been taught. Rabbi Meir
said: that (forbidden) tree from which Adam ate was a vine, for nothing
else but wine brings woe to man.[37]

If the use of fermented wine is one of the evidences of Israel's apostasy
during this period, the prohibitionists missed a good opportunity to
say so and thus remind Israel that their calamity was due to their
drinking fermented wine, assuming that it was not formerly done in
Israel.

Alcohol abuse among the Jews was probably not a large problem
because they drank wine mixed with water—three parts water to one
part wine. This was called *mazug*. We have every reason to believe that
mixing wine with water was not an invention of the Jews of the exile
but goes back to earlier times.[38]

The Jews also drank other beverages, including boiled-down sweet
wine, known as *yayin mebushal*. Sometimes this was used as a jam or
syrup for their bread.

Though they enjoyed many varieties of nonalcoholic drinks, the
people of Israel did drink wine. The Jews, as well as other nations, put
fermented wine in a class by itself. There is no evidence in extra-
biblical literature that *unfermented* wine was considered by the Jews,
Greeks, or Romans as the best wine. The contention that grape juice
was considered the best wine is simply a myth.

37. Ibid.
38. Franz Delitzsch, *Biblical Commentary on the Proverbs of Solomon*, vol. 2, p. 121.

5

Does the Old Testament Prohibit the Use of Alcoholic Beverages?

The Christian's right to drink goes far beyond the matter of rights. The larger issue is the integrity of the Bible, our only authoritative guide to faith and practice. The moment we permit false exegesis in the support of any cause, no matter how noble, we jeopardize the Christian faith.

B. B. Warfield, the great Reformed theologian, saw this years ago, when the opposition to alcohol was at its peak in this country. One historian writes:

> As teetotalism continued to grow, and as some Bible commentators even interpreted the "wine" of Scripture as an unfermented drink, it was not long before grape juice replaced wine in many Baptist, Presbyterian, Disciples, Mennonite, and other evangelical churches. B. B. Warfield, the defender of biblical inerrancy, was one of a small handful to resist this move. Warfield argued that the integrity of the Bible—which did read "wine" and not "grape juice"—was at stake, but his argument had little effect.[1]

---

1. Mark A. Knoll, *Christianity Today*, January 19, 1979, p. 21.

More than anything else, false exegesis of Scripture, including false theories about unfermented wine, have both compromised the integrity of Scripture and discredited an otherwise noble cause—the battle against alcohol abuse.

I have no argument with the prohibitionist's claim that alcohol can be damaging. The examples of Noah, Lot, and others in the Old Testament are too numerous to mention—to say nothing of alcohol abuse in America today. There is no question that God disapproves of alcohol abuse. It is not just a health and social problem. It is a sin.

But the debate is not over alcohol *abuse*. It is over alcohol *use*. The legalistic prohibitionist attempts to prove that *both* alcohol abuse and alcohol use are sins and cites a number of Old Testament references to prove his point.

Passages That Allegedly Prohibit Alcohol

Wine and the Priesthood

One argument that the legalistic prohibitionist frequently offers is that the priests in the Old Testament were forbidden to drink alcohol. Is there any substance to this allegation?

One passage said to prohibit fermented wine is Leviticus 10:8–11:

> Then the LORD said to Aaron, "You and your sons are not to drink wine or other fermented drink whenever you go into the Tent of Meeting, or you will die. This is a lasting ordinance for the generations to come. You must distinguish between the holy and the profane, between the unclean and the clean, and you must teach the Israelites all the decrees the LORD has given them through Moses."

It is alleged that the prohibition against wine or other fermented drink was in force not only while the priests were on duty in the tabernacle but at all other times. According to this view, abstinence was to be a way of life for the priests, as an example for the people. This is based on the statement in verse 10 that the command was given in order to make a distinction between the holy and the profane.

But "the holy and the profane" had to do with the tabernacle as opposed to the rest of the encampment, not to the priests and the people. Nadab and Abihu, anointed priests, had profaned the tabernacle with strange fire (Num. 3:4). The tabernacle was the holy place where an unholy or profane people could meet with a holy God. The priests, by not drinking on duty, bore witness to the fact that the duties performed in the tabernacle were out of the ordinary and required extraordinary behavior not required elsewhere.

Even if we hold that the priests were total abstainers both on and off duty, and as such were set apart from the people, it logically follows that the ordinary people *were* allowed to drink. If they also were total abstainers, then there is no difference between the priests and the people. How, then, does the legalist make a distinction between the holy priests and the profane people according to his interpretation of the passage?

Wine and the Nazirite

Another passage that allegedly prohibits the use of wine in the Old Testament is in Numbers 6, where we are told about the vow of the Nazirite.

Fermented wine—in fact, all grape products—was forbidden the person who took the vow of the Nazirite, a vow of consecration to God. The Nazirite vow is said to argue for the prohibition of fermented wine. But the very prohibition of its use by those taking the vow actually argues for the common use of fermented wine. Because abstinence from alcohol was not the usual custom in Israel, the person who did abstain attracted special attention. This was true not only of the priests on duty but also of the Nazirites.

A Nazirite was any person who took special vows of consecration to God for a specific period. According to Numbers 6, certain restrictions were imposed on the Nazirite during this period of consecration. The vows, in part, included abstinence from *any* product of the grape vine:

. . . If a man or woman wants to make a special vow, a vow of separation to the LORD as a Nazirite, he must abstain from wine and other fermented drink. . . . He must not drink grape juice or eat grapes or raisins. As long as he is a Nazirite, he must not eat anything that comes from the grapevine, not even the seeds or skins [Num. 6:2–4].

After the Nazirite had ended his period of consecration with an appropriate ceremony and offering, he was then permitted to drink wine (Num. 6:19–20).

A number of interesting facts emerge from this passage. First of all, specific products of the vine are identified and distinguished from each other:

wine—*yayin*

other fermented drink or strong drink—*shekar*

vinegar made from wine and strong drink—*chomets*

grape juice—*mishrath-enabiem*

moist (fresh) grapes—*enabiem-lacheim*

dried grapes (raisins)—*enabiem-yabesheim.*

It is clear from this passage that the forbidden fruit included both fermented and nonfermented beverages, as well as other grape-vine products such as fresh grapes and raisins. And among the fermented products were both wine (*yayin*) and strong drink (*shekar*). That these are alcoholic beverages is obvious from the fact that they are distinguished from the nonfermented juice of the grape (*mishrath-enabiem*). The "vinegar" undoubtedly includes vinegar as we know it today—an unfermented food product. It also included sour fermented wine and other sour alcoholic drinks with the generic name *shekar.*[2]

As this passage demonstrates, the Jews had a perfectly good word for grape juice (translated in the Authorized Version as "liquor of grapes"). It would seem that if grape juice was the God-ordained beverage for his people Israel, it would be the word that was used to describe what the Jews drank. Why is it not? Why is *yayin* most frequently used?

The reason is that the people drank the juice of the grape at all stages of production. They drank it as grape juice when it first was expressed, as must in aerobic ferment (sometimes called "new wine"),

---

2. William Younger, *Gods, Men, and Wine*, p. 462.

and as aged wine that went through anaerobic ferment. Because all of these beverages were allowed, it would be most convenient to use a catchall word such as *yayin* to describe what they drank.

Now let us look a little closer at the Nazirite vow. It is clear that the ban on these products was only temporary. The fact that they were banned only during the period of consecration demands that we conclude that *they were at all other times lawful to use.*

Verse 20b removes any question. At the end of the period of consecration, when the Nazirite returned to everyday life, he could return to *all* vinous products: "After that, the Nazirite may drink wine." The word is *yayin*. But what is being permitted here? One writer would have us believe that this granted permission to use unfermented wine only.[3] Are we to believe, then, that grapes, raisins, and vinegar, as well as alcoholic drinks, were still forbidden? This hardly is a satisfactory explanation.

More likely, *yayin* is a generic term for all vinous products. In this passage all vinous products fall under this generic title, as does *shekar*. The obvious intent of the statement in verse 20b is to return the Nazirite to the freedom he had prior to the restrictions imposed by the vow. This would include the freedom to use all the products prohibited in verses 3 and 4—including alcoholic beverages! If it was the intent of God, speaking through Moses, to tell the Nazirite that he could return to everything heretofore prohibited *except alcoholic beverages*, then he was extremely careless in his instructions! Rather than say the former Nazirite may drink *yayin*, he should have said he may drink *mishrath-enabiem*—grape juice.

There is no question that alcoholic beverages are dangerous—that it is possible to be seduced by them. As we shall see, Scripture gives us ample warning about this. But Scripture also makes a distinction between the *use* and *abuse* of alcohol—a distinction that the legalistic prohibitionist refuses to acknowledge.

Samson's Mother and the Nazirite Vow

Another passage often cited is Judges 13:4–7. Samson's mother, who conceived a child who was to be a Nazirite for life, was bound by

---

3. Jack Van Impe, *Alcohol: The Beloved Enemy*, p. 175.

the vow of the Nazirite.[4] But Samson's mother was not required to be a teetotaler all of her life. We are not told whether she remained abstinent only until Samson's birth or for all of his life. But the fact that she was prohibited from drinking alcoholic beverages *after* the conception argues for the fact that she could drink before then. If she never had been allowed to drink fermented wine, why the restriction?

Rulers and Wine

Another argument often raised against the use of alcohol is the prohibition against its use by rulers. Proverbs 31:4–5 is often quoted in this respect:

> "It is not for kings, O Lemuel—
> not for kings to drink wine,
> not for rulers to crave beer,
> lest they drink and forget what the law decrees. . . ."

I would have no trouble going along with the argument that those who rule ought not to drink, strictly on practical grounds. I would like those who make important decisions to be clearheaded. But is this verse arguing for total abstinence or for the importance of moderation, especially for those who rule?

This is an extremely important point and goes back to my concern for the integrity of Scripture. Though I would prefer that those who rule would be total abstainers, does the Bible require it? If it does not, then I better revise my expectations of those who rule rather than revise the Scripture!

The context argues for moderation. In verses 1 through 3 King Lemuel's mother warns him not to spend his strength on women— "those who ruin kings." She probably makes reference to the king's harem, a practice in which the king may lawfully indulge. But perhaps

---

4. The command not to eat anything unclean must also include grapes and raisins, which are proscribed under the Nazirite vow (Num. 6:3). The unclean foods of Leviticus 11 were always forbidden to all Jews. Therefore, Judges 13:6 must refer to this special prohibition binding on the Nazirites.

Lemuel's mother remembers how Solomon's harem led him astray (1 Kings 11:1–8).

It does not sound as though Lemuel's mother is warning him to ignore women completely. It is simply a matter of not making the mistake Solomon made—allowing women to ruin him. If this observation is correct, then the context is introducing the theme of moderation, not abstinence.

She then turns to the matter of alcohol. The warning is not about the *use* of alcohol. As with the women, the warning is in the excessive interest in the perks that the king enjoyed—a harem and banquets.[5] This seems to run parallel with the command in the Pastoral Epistles that elders and deacons are not to be "given to wine." Excessive interest, not use, is what is in view. We will look closer at those passages in chapter 8.

The reason why the ruler is warned against eagerness for his harem and alcohol is that his judgment may be perverted (v. 5). But even if it be argued that this verse is not teaching just moderation for rulers, but abstinence, the text is ambiguous enough to discourage our dogmatizing on the matter. It is a mistake to say that those who rule are sinners and guilty of misfeasance of duty if they drink, even in moderation.

My personal preference is that those who rule or hold high office in government be total abstainers. And I like the idea of pastors being total abstainers for the sake of example. But if a Christian in high office should ask me, "Am I sinning by drinking in moderation?" I must answer that the issue is not clear in this passage. What is clear is that there is no place for immoderate drinking.

This, then, brings us back to the principle of Christian liberty. All things not sinful are lawful, but things that are lawful may not be the smart thing to do—either for our own sake or for the sake of others.

Liberty makes each of us responsible before God. At the same time it protects us from the ecclesiastical tyranny of legalism, which would batter us with condemnation for sins that are not clearly declared sin in Scripture. There is a big difference between what may be

---

5. Franz Delitzsch, *Biblical Commentary on the Proverbs of Solomon*, vol. 2, p. 322.

sinful and what may not be a smart thing to do. The two are not the same. The legalist does not understand this.

Passages That Permit the Use of Alcohol

There are several passages that clearly teach that the use of alcohol is all right. One of them follows the passage just cited.

"Give Beer to the Perishing"

Let us say for sake of argument that a jury of scholars should declare that Proverbs 31:4–5 conclusively teaches that rulers must be total abstainers. That would be fine with me. It would be comforting to know that those who have their finger on the nuclear trigger are clearheaded men or women! But the rest of the proverb seems to leave the door open to the use of alcohol by the common man, particularly those who are distressed:

> Give beer [shekar] to those who are perishing,
>   wine to those who are in anguish;
> let them drink and forget their poverty
>   and remember their misery no more [Prov. 31:6–7].

It may be argued that the proverb is talking about the medicinal use of alcohol. But the proverb speaks of both "misery" and "poverty." Poverty has to do with a broken spirit, not a sick body.

But even prohibitionists are divided on this question. Some say that Paul's urging Timothy to use a little wine for his stomach's sake (1 Tim. 5:23) is an example of medicinal use and is the only instance where fermented wine was approved.[6] Others insist that the "wine" Paul had in mind was not fermented.[7]

The Greeks believed in the medicinal use of wine. Though red wine was regarded with particular caution, amber-colored wine was

6. Van Impe, Alcohol, p. 137.
7. David Wilkerson, Sipping Saints, p. 45.

thought to promote digestion.[8] One of the principal branches of Greco-Roman medicine, *diaetetica* (from which we get our word "dietetics"), prescribed wine. Hippocrates recommended wine of various mixtures. He recommended that a patient suffering great fatigue get himself "drunk" once or twice. But the historian reporting this notes:

> . . . it has been doubted whether actual intoxication is meant or only the "drinking freely and to cheerfulness," in which the same word is used by St. John (ii. 10) and the Septuagint (Gen. xliii. 34; Cant. v. 1; and perhaps Gen. ix. 21).[9]

Though Christians may have the liberty to use alcohol, caution needs to be exercised if we say we are "just using it medicinally." Any time we say we *need* medicine—whether it be a controlled drug, such as a tranquilizer, an anti-depressant, or alcohol—we ought to take it only under the supervision of a doctor.

This may seem like a strange position in view of the fact that I believe Christians have the liberty to drink. Why supervision? A matter of attitude is involved here. Attitude separates alcohol users from abusers. Alcohol users can take it or leave it. Alcohol abusers *need* it. If someone says he needs alcohol medicinally, I would suggest that he receive it by prescription and that it be supervised by a doctor. Or even better, why not have the doctor prescribe a medication that falls under the controlled-substances laws? Then there would be less danger of this need getting out of hand than with alcohol abuse.

---

8. Harry Thurston Peck (ed.), *Harper's Dictionary of Classical Literature and Antiquities*, p. 1662.

9. Ibid., p. 500. This puts an entirely different light on Teachout's "proof" that Ugaritic legends present wine (*yn*) as nonintoxicating grape juice. A weary traveler in one legend is offered *yn*. Teachout (p. 118, "The Use of 'Wine,' in the Old Testament") says that grape juice would be more welcome to the weary traveler than fermented wine because wine is a depressant. But anyone who has had a glass of wine when fatigued understands Hippocrates' prescription for fatigue. Alcohol has a tranquilizing effect on the weary. Unfortunately, many Americans resort to alcohol too frequently and fail to adjust their exhausting way of life.

Alcohol is the only hard drug that is not regulated by controlled-substances laws. As such, it ought to be treated with respect and caution. The Christian who uses alcohol needs to ask some serious questions:

What is my attitude toward alcohol?

Can I take it or leave it, or do I *need* a drink?

Is the "medicinal use" of alcohol a cover-up for my *need* of a hard drug?

Whether or not alcohol ought to be included under the Controlled Substances Act or forbidden entirely by prohibition is a separate issue. The question facing us in Proverbs 31 is whether or not alcohol use is permitted in this proverb. Clearly, the answer is "Yes."

Wine on the Lees

Another passage that permits alcohol use is in Isaiah 25. To understand what Isaiah is saying here we must remember the process of winemaking described in chapter 3. After the grape is crushed, it immediately begins aerobic fermentation. Natural yeast in the juice (or must) immediately begins to interact with the oxygen in the air, converting the sugar into alcohol. After a period of aerobic fermentation, the must is bottled, sealed against air, and anaerobic fermentation begins. Wine is born.

How old the wine gets is determined by how long anaerobic fermentation is permitted to continue. The anaerobic fermentation will stop after a period of time if the container is not disturbed. The wine will "throw" its lees, which settle as sediment at the bottom of the container, leaving "clarified" wine at the top.

The ancients regarded the finest wine to be of this variety. Being "kept on the lees" was the opposite of stirring the lees. This produces a sweet wine. By not stirring the lees, the sugar remaining in the lees is not converted into alcohol. The lees also gave it body (richness of flavor) and color. Not stirring the lees also produced a wine of lower alcohol content.

"Kept on the lees" describes, then, one of the steps in making fine wine. Isaiah refers to this process when he says:

And in this mountain shall the Lord of hosts make unto all people a feast of fat things, a feast of wines on the lees, of fat things full of marrow, of wines on the lees well refined [Isa. 25:6, KJV].

Isaiah sees his people feasting with their God in the coming kingdom. It is a feast of rich foods and "wines on the lees, well refined." This is the kind of wine that I described above. And all Hebrew commentaries I have consulted agree. A typical commentary says:

Shemarim mezukkakim are wines which have been left to stand upon their lees [dregs or sediment] after the first ferment is over, which have thus thoroughly fermented and which have been kept a long time (from shamar, to keep,) spec. to allow to ferment, and which then are filtered before the drinking . . . , hence the wine is both strong and clear.[10]

But prohibitionists disagree with this commentary. They say that shemarim, which comes from the root shamar, has the general signification of things preserved.[11] So far so good. But what is being preserved? The prohibitionist says that the pure juice of the grape is being preserved against fermentation! Such a statement is incredible, given the chemistry of winemaking and the unanimous consensus of Hebrew lexicographers and Bible translators.

One Hebrew lexicon, widely used by evangelical scholars, plainly says, ". . . shemarim, m. dregs (of wine), so called because, when wine is kept on the lees, its strength and color are preserved [emphasis mine]."[12] The keeping and preserving have nothing to do with preventing grape juice from becoming wine but with the common practice of keeping it on the lees to achieve full body. This is wine that is undisturbed after the first ferment is complete.

10. Delitzsch, Biblical Commentary on the Prophecies of Isaiah, vol. 1, p. 439.

11. Van Impe, Alcohol, p. 173.

12. Samuel Prideaux Tregelles, Gesenius' Hebrew and Chaldee Lexicon to the Old Testament Scriptures, p. 838.

This meaning is illustrated in two other Old Testament passages. Jeremiah uses the word *shamar* in connection with winemaking to illustrate a quiet and tranquil life:

> "Moab has been at rest from youth,
>   like wine left on its dregs,
> not poured from one jar to another—
>   she has not gone into exile" [Jer. 48:11].

This is wine whose first ferment has quieted down and is not disturbed and reactivated by pouring from one jar to another.

The prophet Zephaniah records *shamar* as a metaphor of complacency:

> "At that time I will search Jerusalem with lamps
>   and punish those who are complacent,
>   who are like wine left on dregs . . ." [Zeph. 1:12].

In both cases the word describes those who refuse to stir themselves to action, as wine that is unstirred after its first ferment. The idea of grape juice kept from fermentation is foreign to the text and the chemistry of winemaking.

Isaiah in the passage quoted above (25:6) sees God feasting with his people—not on grape juice but on fine, clarified wine of low alcohol content. God gives his people only the *best* wine. It is "well refined." After the lees settle they are "racked off."[13] Both siphoning and straining were used in ancient times to produce a clear wine.[14] This kind of wine was so prized by the Babylonians that they paid eight times more for fermented, racked grape wine than for ordinary date wine.[15]

---

13. Ibid.

14. Younger, *Gods, Men, and Wine*, pp. 48, 62.

15. Ibid., p. 62.

An Important Contradiction

Before leaving the word *shemarim*, I should point out that legalistic prohibitionists not only misinterpret the word, they are guilty of a serious contradiction in their own writings when they use this word.[16]

One book, popular among prohibitionists, tells us that Psalm 75 warns us against the use of fermented wine, which is pictured as a symbol of God's wrath. This psalm says in verse 8 (NASB):

> For a cup is in the hand of the LORD, and the wine foams;
> It is well mixed, and He pours out of this;
> Surely all the wicked of the earth must drain and drink down its dregs
>   [*shamar*].

Here the author understands *shamar* to have reference to fermented wine—and properly so, for the reasons I have discussed above.

But in another place the same author, quoting another writer on the word *shamar,* says that it means "preserved," suggesting that the beverage had never become fermented wine, but was preserved as grape juice. And Psalm 78:8 *is cited!* On one page he declares that the wine is fermented; on another it is not.

I do not point out this contradiction to embarrass, but only to illustrate what I have been contending all along. Though the Bible is very clear that alcohol *abuse* is wrong, it is not clear that alcohol *use* is wrong. And when men on the same side cannot agree, they must not be dogmatic.

The first interpretation of Psalm 75:8 in the book mentioned above is the correct one. Fermented red wine whose dregs have been stirred or "well mixed" is an appropriate symbol of God's wrath. It is strong and capable of bringing down the strongest of men. It therefore must be used cautiously, or not at all if the drinker's attitude toward drinking is wrong (Prov. 23:31).

Though God permits the use of alcohol, we are to use it cautiously and responsibly. This is basic to the exercise of liberty—and the answer to the warnings about alcohol in the next chapter.

_____

16. Van Impe, *Alcohol*, pp. 108, 173.

6

Let the User Beware

Intoxicating wine mocks, impoverishes, affects health,
injures its users, and contributes to immorality and
dishonesty. It warps character, encouraging selfishness
and greed. It is seen as a symbol of God's wrath and
judgment. [1]

The statement above is representative of the legalistic
view of alcoholic beverages. It refuses to distinguish between alcohol
use, permitted under liberty with caution, and alcohol *abuse*, which is
prohibited by Scripture. Legalists consider all the Old Testament
passages that warn about wine and strong drink as prohibitions
against their use, rather than as warnings about their abuse. This is
most unfortunate, because it robs us of a proper biblical perspective.

In this chapter we shall examine the warnings against alcohol in
the Old Testament. We are told three things: (1) it is dangerous when

---

1. Jack Van Impe, *Alcohol: The Beloved Enemy*, p. 109.

we have a wrong attitude; (2) it is dangerous when we underestimate its power; and (3) it is a symbol of God's wrath.

The Danger of Wrong Attitude

One of the well-known warnings is in Proverbs 23:31, where we are told not to gaze upon the wine "when it is red." This warning is part of the larger passage, Proverbs 23:29–35, where Solomon issues a warning to alcohol users about the danger of a wrong attitude toward alcohol:

> Who has woe? Who has sorrow?
>   Who has strife? Who has complaints?
>   Who has needless bruises? Who has bloodshot eyes?
> Those who linger over wine,
>   who go to sample bowls of mixed wine.
> Do not gaze at wine when it is red,
>   when it sparkles in the cup,
>   when it goes down smoothly!
> In the end it bites like a snake
>   and poisons like a viper.
> Your eyes will see strange sights
>   and your mind imagine confusing things.
> You will be like one sleeping on the high seas,
>   lying on top of the rigging.
> "They hit me," you will say, "but I'm not hurt!
>   They beat me, but I don't feel it!
> When will I wake up
>   so I can find another drink?"

Two types of problem drinkers are identified in this passage: "Those who linger over wine, who go to sample bowls of mixed wine" (v. 30) and those who "gaze at wine when it is red, when it sparkles in the cup, when it goes down smoothly!" (v. 31).

Lingering and Sampling

The first type of problem drinker reveals his wrong attitude in his "lingering" and "sampling." This is the person who goes out looking for the wine houses, the places of revelry, where he can find the stiffest drink. The purpose of his sampling the bowls of mixed wine is to test the proportion of wine to water.[1] Does the tavern-keeper water down the wine so much that the patrons can't get a decent "buzz" on, or can they get a substantial drink?

This man's attitude toward alcohol is wrong because he is drinking with the intention of getting drunk. This type of drinker is like those described by Isaiah the prophet when he said, "Woe to those who are heroes at drinking wine and champions at mixing drinks" (Isa. 5:22). Isaiah had in mind a type of drinker that we see even in our day—the person who sees drinking as a competitive sports event. He is interested in finding out who can drink the most and stay on his feet.

Longing for the Red Wine

The color of wine, to the ancients, was a criterion for its strength. "Black" or dark red wine was the strongest, as is the case today.[2] There is good reason for this. The skins of dark grapes steep and ferment with the juice of the grapes to add pigment, acid, and body, while white wine ferments only the flesh of the grape. This is one reason why white wine tends to be "lighter" than red wine. We have seen that red wine, left on the lees, offers an opportunity for longer fermentation. And from time to time the container is agitated to activate latent fermentation.

Another reason for the high alcohol content of red wine is the relatively high sugar content of red grapes. Since yeast converts grape sugar into alcohol, the higher the sugar content of the grapes, the higher the alcohol content of the finished wine. This is why winos prefer muscatel, made from a very sweet, red grape that produces a wine high in alcohol content.

The proverb instructs us not to "long" or "lust after" this kind of wine. I have found that one of the patterns of alcohol abuse today begins in this type of situation. Drinkers often will begin with light white or rosé wine, anywhere from 6 to 8 percent alcohol. After a

---

1. Franz Delitzsch, *Biblical Commentary on the Proverbs of Solomon*, vol. 2, p. 121.

2. Harry Thurston Peck (ed.), *Harper's Dictionary of Classical Literature and Antiquities*, p. 1662.

while, to get more of a kick, they will move on to the more potent reds. There is such a brand on the market today, a cheap item called Red Lady, very dark and potent—20 percent alcohol.

Another quality of this dangerous wine is its "sparkle." Neither effervescence nor fermentation is meant here. The reference is to its color and the movement of the color, which is one of the pleasures wine drinkers find in their wine. The richness of the red speaks of its strength and ability to intoxicate easily—the very thing that draws the drinker in the first place.

From the pleasure of the eye the proverb moves to the pleasure of the palate. This dangerous wine "goes down smoothly." The serious drinker prizes this quality in a drink. It is powerful, but it goes down smoothly. Smoothness is a quality sought not only in strong wine but also in modern distilled spirits.

Note how often liquor ads praise this quality. Jack Daniels 90-proof whiskey is "charcoal mellowed drop by drop." B & B, a cordial is described as "delicate" and "fine." Six-year-old Seagram's V.O. whiskey is "unexpectedly smooth, surprisingly light"—and more potent than any ancient reveler could have imagined. Though it may go down smoothly, the bite comes the next day with the hangover and other consequences of gross intoxication (vv. 32–35).

But before the prohibitionist takes up a hatchet to go out and break up saloons, he or she should go back to Proverbs 23:19–21 and note the immediate context that introduces this subject. The context is dealing with *intemperance of every sort*. The glutton, the ravenous person, is condemned along with the drunkard.

There is nothing quite so incongruous as an overweight prohibitionist railing against the evil of alcohol. The excuse often offered by the intemperate eater is that his problem is not overeating: "It's a glandular problem." But rarely is overweight the result of malfunctioning glands, unless, of course, they are overactive *salivary* glands.

Overeaters Anonymous, founded in 1960 to help people with intemperate eating habits, patterned its program after Alcoholics Anonymous because it saw that the overeater has the same problem as the alcohol abuser. Overeaters have lost control of their eating and need to begin with the same confession required of alcohol abusers—the confession that their behavior in this regard is beyond their control.

The legalist is correct in saying that ". . . some people, wanting to justify themselves, assume that gluttony and drunkenness are sins of the same kind, that they are 'equally serious' before God."[3] But I have no such motive. My problem with this kind of distinction is the hypocrisy of it, which is typical of legalism.

The Jewish legalists in the New Testament were roundly condemned for this kind of hypocrisy again and again. They would minimize or excuse one sin while they condemned another (Matt. 23:16–21). The Bible speaks of the sin of gluttony four times and always names it along with drunkenness.

Gluttony, like drunkenness, begins with a wrong attitude toward a good thing. Gluttony, like drunkenness, brings premature death to countless numbers of people. It precipitates heart disease, high blood pressure, and stroke. Gluttony, like drunkenness, is an insidious disease because it takes its toll so gradually that its effects are not noticeable until the body has been damaged. Gluttons and drunkards have this in common: a wrong attitude toward food and drink.

The Danger of Underestimating Alcohol's Power

Another important warning in the Old Testament concerns alcohol's power. The warning in Proverbs 20:1 goes beyond merely avoiding especially strong drinks; it applies to all alcoholic beverages:

> Wine is a mocker and beer a brawler;
> whoever is led astray by them is not wise.

Wine is a Mocker

Wine (*yayin*) is personified here, and as such is described as a creature who mocks, one who derides others and mocks them by imitating their voice. The writer is describing what happens when we surrender the control of our person to the control of this other "person," wine. The degree to which we surrender control is the degree to which wine is able to perform on our stage as a mocking buffoon.

---

3. Robert P. Teachout, *Wine The Biblical Imperative: Total Abstinence*, p. 77.

The prophet Isaiah gives an excellent illustration of this. In his day the rulers of Judah, which included the priests, had begun to abuse alcohol. Things had gotten so bad that they were intoxicated in the midst of prophetic visions and when passing judicial sentences.[4] Isaiah attempted to reason with them but was rebuffed in a manner typical of alcohol abusers. In Isaiah 28:9–10 the drunken priests, feeling that Isaiah was talking down to them, say:

> "Who is it he is trying to teach?
>   To whom is he explaining his message?
> To children weaned from their milk,
>   to those just taken from the breast?
> For it is:
>   Do and do, do and do,
>   rule on rule, rule on rule
>   a little here, a little there."

This might be paraphrased, "Who does Isaiah think he is teaching, anyway? Who does he think he's instructing? Does he think that we're little children just weaned from mother's milk, that he has to guide our little fingers precept by precept through the law or guide our little hands in forming each letter of the alphabet? 'Now make this line like this and that line like that. And this is the way the letters sound: *tzav, latzav, tzav latzav, qav laqav, qav laqav.*'" This mockery expresses the scorn of the priests toward Isaiah. But it is the wine that is speaking.[5]

The proverb offers excellent insight into the psychology of the drunkard—behavior that is well known to those who work with alcohol abusers. *There is no reasoning with the alcohol abuser and alcoholic.* And this is true not only when the wine is talking. It is true even in the alcohol abuser's moments of sobriety. The more frequently and the more completely we yield ourselves to *yayin*, the more we become a personification of wine, the permanent performer on our stage.

---

4. Delitzsch, *Biblical Commentary on the Prophecies of Isaiah*, vol. 2, p. 6.

5. The Rev. A. R. Fausset, *A Commentary, Critical, Experimental, and Practical, of the Old and New Testaments*, vol. 3, p. 648.

Beer Is a Brawler

The proverb goes on to say that beer (*shekar*) is a brawler. This does not mean that wine does one thing and beer does something else. This is an example of parallelism in Hebrew poetry. The idea of the first line is expanded on by the second.

"Beer" is a translation of the Hebrew word *shekar*, which covers more than beer. It also includes a drink made of pomegranates (Song of Sol. 8:2). Hard cider and mead were also given this name. Mead is an alcoholic beverage made of fermented honey and water, often mixed with spices, fruit, and malt.

When *shekar* is compared to *yayin* (wine), it is often translated "strong drink" to indicate its more potent quality. The Hebrew word *shekar* probably came from the Sumerian *sikaru* meaning "strong drink," which had particular reference to an exceptionally potent date wine known to give the drinker a headache.[6]

The proverb warns that *shekar* is "a brawler." It makes the drinker agitated and noisy.[7] This is the same word that describes the adulterous woman in Proverbs 7:11—the woman who is loud and defiant. Internally and externally she is impetuous. When drunk, this person is called "uninhibited."

The warning is the same as it is with the wine: surrender to *shekar* and you assuredly will be agitated, noisy, and uninhibited. By including *yayin* and *shekar* together, Solomon intends to include all alcoholic beverages in his warning. And what exactly is the warning? "Whoever is led astray by them is not wise." *Yayin* and *shekar* have the ability to produce unacceptable behavior. Experience certainly reinforces what the proverb says.

But what does it mean to be "led astray"? Do alcoholic beverages have some kind of mysterious power? From my personal experience and from the experience of my clients with alcohol problems, I have come to the conclusion that alcohol does have a great deal of power to lead astray. I believe it is the most seductive drug there is.

---

6. William Younger, *Gods, Men, and Wine*, p. 56.
7. Prof. Karl Feyerabend, *Langenscheidt's Hebrew-English Dictionary to the Old Testament*, p. 78.

Those who drink on a regular basis develop a tolerance for alcohol. Over the years it takes more and more alcohol to produce the desired effect. This effect often leaves chronic drinkers with a false sense of security. Rather than see their growing tolerance for alcohol as a sign of trouble, they proudly take it as evidence that they can handle their alcohol.

As the amount of alcohol ingested grows over the years, addiction slowly sets in. For some it is psychological addiction—I call these people "alcohol abusers." For others it is physiological addiction— these people are true "alcoholics." But the process is so slow that the drinker is often unaware that it is happening. When he finally has his first major warning, such as a blackout, he may become alarmed and quit drinking completely. But even this is deceptive. The drinker has probably not yet become so addicted that he has any noticeable withdrawal symptoms, as one might experience with other hard drugs. He may go two or three weeks without a drink and finally decide that the blackout was no big deal. And what is more, he says, "Why should I worry about alcohol? Wasn't it easy to quit? Doesn't that prove I'm not an alcoholic or alcohol abuser?"

He thinks he can break off his relationship with alcohol, as he might with a woman, anytime he wants and resume complete control of his life. But alcohol is a seductive creature. She knows that if she waits patiently he will come back.

Wine, like a woman, can be delightful if she is not the man's master. But if he foolishly surrenders himself to her and makes her his life, she is capable of possessing him and destroying him. This analogy suits quite well the words of King Lemuel's mother in Proverbs 31:1–5. A man may love a woman and have his wine. But he must always remember that both of these delightful creatures have the ability to ruin the man who makes them his whole life.[9] We are not to lose our

---

9. This statement reveals my view of love and marriage as well as my view of drinking. It's a mistake for a man or woman to lose self completely in marriage and cease being an individual. Not only does this person, by giving up his identity, manifest neurotic behavior, he also encourages possessiveness in the spouse. The mathematics of marriage are not $1 + 1 = 1$, but $1 + 1 = 3$. They are one couple but still two individuals.

identity to either a lover or to wine—though both are a delight. (For more on alcohol addiction and recovery, see Appendix A.)

Get Smart

Proverbs 20:1 tells us something else that is very enlightening. The person who unwisely surrenders himself completely to alcohol is said to be "not wise." This is curious. Why doesn't it say that the person is a *sinner*?

The answer is found in the fact that sin in the Bible has both moral and practical consequences. A holy God has created us and the world in such a way that his holiness is expressed in the laws that regulate both the physical world and human nature. Drunkenness is not only a sin against a holy God whose character is alien to drunkenness. Drunkenness is not smart! The person who repeatedly and consistently gets drunk finds that he cannot live successfully in a society of fellow humans created in God's image or on this planet created by God. Why is this? Even though the drunkard might turn his back on a holy God and disregard the sin question, he still must live on God's earth and cooperate with the laws by which God runs his world.

The Book of Proverbs is concerned with holiness and sin, but it tends to deal with the "practical" side of holiness. Avoiding sin is not only the "spiritual" thing to do; it is also the smart thing to do! This is why the Book of Proverbs opens with the statement, "The fear of the LORD is the beginning of knowledge . . ." (Prov. 1:7).

This concept is important to remember when dealing with alcoholics and alcohol abusers. More often than not they couldn't care less that they are sinners. But they cannot avoid the fact that they are not being smart. The inflexible laws of God's creation remind them of it every day they abuse alcohol.

One of the difficulties we have in coping with the seductive power of alcohol is that the alcoholic beverage industry attempts to disarm our caution. I mention this because a comprehensive solution to alcoholism and alcohol abuse does not belong to the individual alone. It belongs to society at large. Dr. Morris E. Chafetz, past director of the National Institute for Alcoholism and Alcohol Abuse (NIAAA), once said, "It is a basic principle of medicine that no condition is brought under control by treating the casualties alone."[10]

A Symbol of God's Wrath

Wine in the Bible is frequently used as a symbol of God's wrath. Prohibitionists maintain that this symbolism provides an argument against alcohol use and cite several passages of Scripture as examples.

In Psalm 60:3 God's judgment on his people is compared to having potent wine forced on them, wine that makes them "stagger." Psalm 75:8 makes a similar statement. Here, a powerful wine, of the nature described in Proverbs 23:31, is forced upon the people. They are forced to drink it to the very dregs without stopping. Jeremiah uses similar imagery. The wine of God's wrath sends the nations staggering (Jer. 25:15–16).

What are we to make of this? Are we to conclude that we should not use wine because it is connected with God's wrath? Not at all! These proverbs actually reinforce what is said about wine in Proverbs 23. We are being warned that wine can be dangerous, particularly the potent red wine. This potent wine has the ability to produce damage that is like the wrath of God itself!

A look at the results of alcohol abuse should convince any doubters:

25,000 die annually in alcohol-related traffic accidents.

650,000 people are injured annually in alcohol-related traffic accidents.

80% of murders, 70% of assaults, 60% of child-abuse incidents, 50% of rapes, 50% of deaths by fire and drowning, 40% of home accidents, and 33% of suicides are alcohol-related.[11]

---

10. Louise Bailey Burgess, *Alcohol and Your Health*, p. 157.

11. *World Almanac and Book of Facts*, 1984, and *Statistical Abstracts*, 1984.

Dr. William C. Menninger once said, "If alcoholism were a communicable disease, a national emergency would be declared."[12]

Potent wine is indeed an appropriate symbol of God's wrath. But the symbolism is not an argument for abstinence, though some of us have been frightened enough by our encounter with alcohol to do just that! It is an argument for caution. Though its use is permitted by the Bible and by most cultures, those societies with the smallest incidence of alcoholism and alcohol abuse obviously treat it with great respect!

The Old Testament, in warning us about alcoholic beverages does just this. We may be permitted to use alcohol, but we must use it with caution!

---

12. Burgess, *Alcohol and Your Health*, p. 9.

7

Jesus and Wine

The idea that Jesus had anything to do with fermented wine is unthinkable to many Christians. Yet there is ample evidence in the Gospels that he actually approved of fermented wine. It is found in the following New Testament themes:

1. *Putting New Wine in Old Wineskins* (Matt. 9:17; Mark. 2:22; Luke 5:36–39)
2. *Jesus Came Eating and Drinking* (Matt. 11:19; Luke 7:33–34)
3. *Turning Water into Wine* (John 2:3–10)
4. *The Last Supper* (Matt. 26:27–29; Mark 14:23–25; Luke 22:17–20)
5. *Wine Offered to Jesus at the Crucifixion* (Matt. 27:32–55; Mark 15:23).

Putting New Wine in Old Wineskins

He [Jesus] told them this parable: "No one tears a patch from a new garment and sews it on an old one. If he does, he will have torn the new garment, and the patch from the new will not match the old. And no one pours new wine into old wineskins. If he does, the new wine will burst the skins, the wine will run out and the wineskins will be ruined. No, new wine must be poured into new wineskins. And no one

68

after drinking old wine wants the new, for he says, 'The old is better.' "
[Luke 5:36–39].

Those who believe that the "wine" used by believers in Old and New
Testament times was unfermented maintain that we have here another evidence of preserving wine without fermentation.

The purpose of putting new wine in new wineskins is, according to
the prohibitionist view, "to keep the new, unfermented wine sweet and
non alcoholic as long as possible."[1] It is argued that the new skin was
sought for its cleanliness. But such an interpretation cannot be supported by the passage, as we shall see.

The Parable's Meaning

John the Baptist's disciples had a problem. They wanted to know
why they and the Pharisees fasted and Jesus' disciples did not (Matt.
9:14). Jesus answered with the parable of the wineskins. He tells them
that there was a good reason why his disciples did not follow tradition.
The liberty and joy of Christianity was incompatible with the legalism
and self-mortification of Judaism. Jesus is telling the disciples of John
that if they are to move from the legalism of Judaism to the grace and
joy of Christianity, a patchwork solution would not do. Indeed, it
would make matters worse. If they patch an old garment with a piece
of new, unshrunk cloth, the new cloth will shrink when the garment is
washed and will make the tear worse. If they try to put new wine in old
wineskins that have lost their stretch, the skins will burst when the
wine ferments and the carbon dioxide builds up. Nothing short of
complete change would do. The customs and traditions of Judaism
had to be set aside.

The cleanliness of the wineskins is not the concern here. It is the
new skin's ability to stretch under the pressure of fermentation that
Jesus alludes to. The parable of the new cloth illustrates a similar
principle. We are dealing with the properties of shrinking and stretch-
ing in this parable, properties common to that which is new.

---

1. Jack Van Impe, *Alcohol: The Beloved Enemy*, p. 121.

Winemaking Not Understood by the Prohibitionist

Cleanliness is not the issue here. The prohibitionist once again shows that he does not understand the chemistry of fermentation when he says,

> The new bottles or skins, being clean and perfectly free from all ferment, were essential for preserving the fresh unfermented juice, not that their strength might resist the force of fermentation, but, being clean and free from fermenting matter, and closely tied and sealed, so as to exclude the air, the wine would be preserved in the same state in which it was put into those skins.[2]

The prohibitionist points out that Columella's recipe for keeping the wine "always sweet" expressly directs that the newest must be put in a "new amphora," or jar.[3] But this does not argue for the preservation of grape juice in an unfermented state. Must cannot be kept from fermenting, even when immersed in water.

In the first place, it was impossible to keep airborne yeast out of the must when bottling. The idea that no fermenting matter went into the bottle is absurd. They did use sulfur to clean their receptacles, but this controlled bacteria. It also promoted the growth of the hardy wine yeast.

In the second place, the idea of excluding air so the wine would be preserved in the same state in which it was put in those skins is also absurd. Air was not totally excluded. The skins were porous. And even if anaerobic conditions (absence of free oxygen) were guaranteed, this would have been the ideal condition for making good aged wine. It would also keep it from being contaminated by the vinegar fly. Whether the wine fermented aerobically (with air present) or anaerobically (under sealed conditions), *it still fermented.*

Columella's recipe for keeping wine "always sweet" is a recipe to keep it from turning to vinegar, not a recipe for keeping juice from turning into wine.

------

2. Ibid.
3. Ibid.

Jesus Came Eating and Drinking

Another passage that often provokes debate about drinking is in Luke 7, where the Pharisees accuse Jesus of being a glutton and drunkard:

"To what, then, can I compare the people of this generation? What are they like? They are like children sitting in the marketplace and calling out to each other:

"'We played the flute for you,
  and you did not dance;
we sang a dirge,
  and you did not cry.'"

For John the Baptist came neither eating bread nor drinking wine, and you say, 'He has a demon.' The Son of Man came eating and drinking, and you say, 'Here is a glutton and a drunkard, a friend of tax collectors and "sinners."' But wisdom is proved right by all her children" [Luke 7:31–34].

The Pharisees' Unreasonableness

Jesus was here attempting to show the unreasonableness of the Pharisees, who thought John the Baptist was too austere and Jesus was too genial. The Pharisees were like children playing a game of charades where one group would act out a part and the other group would guess what the charade was. It was bad enough the religious leaders acted like children; but worse, they acted like petulant children. They acted out a marriage, but John the Baptist would not dance to their flute. They acted out a funeral for Jesus, but he didn't play with them and join in their wailing.[4]

It certainly is not true that Jesus was a glutton and drunkard. He is the sinless Son of God. But it *is* true that he could relate to self-confessed sinners in such a warm, loving manner that he ingratiated

---

4. David Smith, *The Days of His Flesh*, p. 228.

himself to them. This is seen, for example, in the way Jesus related to the sinful woman who anointed him (Luke 7:36–50).

A Friend of Sinners

One of the ways Jesus won over the Publicans and sinners was to eat and drink with them. This much is true (Matt. 9:9–13; Luke 19:1–10). We cannot know conclusively whether or not he drank alcoholic beverages on these occasions, but he must have had what was the customary drink. This would have been *homez*, the drink of the common person—a poor-quality wine made of water and the wine dregs from the last rinsing of the vat. Its alcoholic content would have been very low.

When entertained by wealthy tax collectors like Matthew and Zacchaeus, a better wine undoubtedly was on the bill of fare. But to suggest that Jesus drank only grape juice is impossible to believe, particularly when it was not the season of grape harvest and there was no handy grape press offering fresh juice. Though it is quite possible that Jesus drank a nonintoxicating beverage, I find it difficult to believe that the sinners he drank with were teetotalers.

Wine was one of the customary drinks of the Jews in these days. Even legalists admit this, citing it as one of the evidences of their apostasy. But if wine drinking was so reprehensible to God, why did Jesus not use these occasions of eating and drinking together as opportunities to point out this most heinous sin? What is more, if others drank wine and Jesus did not, his example would have been enough to make the charge of drunkenness ridiculous.

The Pharisees were right about one thing. Jesus was not austere. And he was the friend of sinners. But as typical legalists, the Pharisees condemned any association of Jesus with sinners as evidence of his own sinfulness.

Don't Major on Minors

One problem legalists always have had, both in Jesus' day and in our own, is that they find it difficult to be friends of sinners. Paul's first letter to the Corinthians gives us some instruction along this line.

Paul had already made it clear to the Corinthians that Christian liberty permitted them to eat meat that came from an idolatrous sacrifice, so long as it was no offense to themselves or to a weaker Christian. But what happens when mingling with an unbeliever? Paul says,

> If some unbeliever invites you to a meal and you want to go, eat whatever is put before you without raising questions of conscience. But if anyone says to you, "This has been offered in sacrifice," then do not eat it, both for the sake of the man who told you and for con- science' sake—the other man's conscience, I mean, not yours. For why should my freedom be judged by another's conscience? If I take part in the meal with thankfulness, why am I denounced because of some- thing I thank God for? [1 Cor. 10:27–30].

Since the Corinthian Christians had social contacts with unbelievers, it was possible that by accepting an invitation to dinner they might wind up eating steaks from a butchered heathen sacrifice. What were they to do? They were to eat without raising questions of conscience. The reference is to the host's conscience. If the host sees nothing wrong with a Christian's eating meat from an idolatrous sacrifice, the Christian is not to raise the issue. On debatable matters or matters of scruples, we are not to make an issue over something that is not an issue to the other person.

Sin is a completely different matter. Though a particular sin may not be an issue to the unbeliever, it is an issue to the Christian. Sin has nothing to do with how we feel about it. It is not a "disputable" matter (Rom. 14:1). But the case in point has nothing to do with sin. It deals with scruples or debatable issues. *We are not to make an issue with the unbeliever over debatable things.*

Many years ago I was faced with a situation exactly like this. In 1950 I was in the Air Force and stationed in Japan. Several of my Christian buddies and I, using a Japanese seminary student as an interpreter, held evangelistic meetings at the police academy in Fukuoka. We and our message were well received. The police superintendent was most gracious to us, and when we received our orders to fly home, he asked if he might have a banquet in our honor before we left.

The meal was specially prepared at the academy and was a grand feast. The superintendent treated us royally. He started out the meal by having waiters come around and fill each of our glasses with beer. Then the superintendent said, "I want to toast my honored guests who have been such a help to my men." He raised his glass and nodded to us as if to say, "Will you drink to that?"

The Baptist seminary student looked as though he could have died! I knew what his problem was. This devout Baptist would not let alcohol touch his lips. He put his hands together, as if in prayer, bowed deeply, and would not look at the superintendent, who was dumbfounded. Undoubtedly he wondered why his honored guests would not join in his toast.

I quickly picked up my glass, raised it in toast, and took a sip. My buddies followed suit, but the seminarian just remained bowed.

The incident spoiled what was otherwise a good relationship with the superintendent. I was deeply distressed, and even to this day it distresses me to think about it. It did not help the cause of Christ but rather diverted attention from the gospel to beer! This is what Paul is getting at in his letter to the Corinthians. Don't make an issue over a non-issue—something that is debatable rather than a matter of sin.

But suppose the host at a banquet *does* make an issue over the food and drink. Suppose he says, "I forgot. You are a Christian, and I'm sure that you don't want to eat meat that came from a sacrifice to Zeus." In that case, the Christian must leave the meat alone and just eat his salad and potato. Why? Because of the *other man's* conscience. If an unbeliever sees the behavior as unsuitable for a Christian, then we ought to respect his conscience on the matter.

Someone may ask, "Why should I be kept from eating a perfectly good steak just because this unbeliever thinks I shouldn't?" (v. 30). The answer is clear:

> So whether you eat or drink or whatever you do, do it all for the glory of God. Do not cause anyone to stumble, whether Jews, Greeks or the church of God—even as I try to please everybody in every way. For I am not seeking my own good but the good of many, so that they may be saved. Follow my example, as I follow the example of Christ [1 Cor. 10:31–33].

Food and drink, which is neutral in itself, should be handled in a way that glorifies God and is not an offense to others. It can be an offense if we refuse to eat and drink certain items, and it can be an offense if we do eat and drink others. On debatable issues we must decide how God will be best glorified.

This is not situation ethics, which teaches that we may *sin* if the situation calls for that response. Christian liberty does not teach this at all. It deals with debatable issues, not sin.

The Miracle at Cana

The miracle at Cana, where Jesus turned water into wine, raises more debate than any other event. Did Jesus really turn water into fermented wine? The miracle is recorded in John 2:1–11. There the master of the banquet called Jesus' wine the best:

> . . . the master of the banquet tasted the water that had been turned into wine. He did not realize where it had come from, though the servants who had drawn the water knew. Then he called the bridegroom aside and said, "Everyone brings out the choice wine first and then the cheaper wine after the guests have had too much to drink; but you have saved the best till now" [John 2:9–10].

The Best Wine

In chapter 4 we saw that the "best" wine to those living in these days was not grape juice. Indeed, inferior wine was not subject to the prescribed year of aerobic fermentation. The must of the inferior "wine" was drunk at all stages: fresh from the press, and as "new wine" at all stages of aerobic fermentation.

The best wine was aged wine. It would have been quite a miracle if Jesus had made the most famous wine of all—the 100-year-old *vinum Opimianum*, which was still being drunk in those days.[5]

Were the Guests Drunk?

The moral and ethical difficulties of the miracle are laid to rest by the fact that the master of the banquet was to see to it that the wine

---

5. Harry Thurston Peck (ed.), *Harper's Dictionary of Classical Literature and Antiquities*, p. 1662.

was liberally diluted with water. This was one of the duties of the master.[6] This does not mean that the mixed wine was nonintoxicating. Indeed, the master of the banquet was surprised at the fine quality of the wine coming so late in the feast, "after the guests have had too much to drink" (John 2:10).

The guests were not drunk, however. The expression "too much to drink" is the Greek word *methuo*, meaning "to soften with drink." Though the word usually means "drunk," it can refer to anything from "cheerfulness" to gross intoxication. If John wanted to leave no doubt that these people were drunk he could have used the word *oinophlugia* (excess, or overflowing with wine) or he could have identified the people as *oinopotes*—drunkards. He says they are *methuo*. They are sated. Their palates have had enough food and drink to be satisfied and really could not appreciate the good wine that Jesus made.

Just exactly how much alcohol did these people drink? We can make an educated guess by using today's legal criterion of drunkenness, which is a blood-alcohol level above .05 percent. This would mean that they did not drink more than five to ten ounces of 12 percent wine per hour, though it would vary according to the drinker's weight (see Appendix B).

The Last Supper

When Jesus instituted the ordinance of communion at the Last Supper, he used language that some believe is evidence that he used the unfermented juice of the grape in the memorial. In Matthew 26 Jesus said, "I tell you I will not drink of this fruit of the vine until I drink it anew with you in my father's kingdom" (Matt. 26:29).

The Fruit of the Vine

Earlier in the ceremony Jesus referred only to the cup (v. 27). Prohibitionists therefore conclude that fermented wine is out of the question. They say that fermented wine certainly cannot be considered the fruit of the vine. One writer, arguing this position, says,

6. Ibid.

Fermented wine is not a product of the vine. Chemically it is entirely different from the sweet and unfermented grape juice. Fermented wine is 14% alcohol, and it has other constituents that are not found in the fresh grape juice. Alcohol does not grow on the vine. It is not a vine product. Alcohol is the product of decay, the product of fermentation. It is produced by the process of spoiling.[7]

Note that the legalist connects wine with decay and spoiling. To him wine is therefore not an appropriate symbol for the blood of Christ. He argues, "Fermented wine, with microbes of decay, would not picture the perfect blood of a sinless Christ."[8] The legalist argues that since it was prophesied that Jesus would see no corruption ("decay") (Ps. 16:10), "corrupted" grape juice would be an inappropriate symbol.

When the legalist speaks this way about wine he once again shows his ignorance of the chemistry of wine. In chapter 3 we saw that wine is not connected with death and decay. It is connected with *life*. When must becomes true wine, it undergoes anaerobic fermentation, which is life without free oxygen.

The Argument of Leaven

Because leavened bread was excluded from the memorial, or from any sacrifice for that matter, legalists sometimes argue that wine, a product of ferment like leaven, would be an unsuitable sacrifice. But this is an argument from silence.

We are not told why fermented wine was permitted in the sacrificial system and not leavened bread. It may involve nothing more than the nature of bread and fruit juice. Unleavened bread was easier to keep than unfermented grape juice. This was a practical matter, since the bread offered in the tabernacle was to be continually before the Lord as "Bread of the Presence." Every Sabbath the priests would go into the holy place with fresh bread offered by the Israelites. There amid the rising clouds of incense they would eat the week-old bread in communion with God. But there is no mention of drink being part of that communion meal (Lev. 24:5–9).

---

7. Van Impe, *Alcohol*, pp. 126–27.
8. Ibid.

Bread without yeast stood in God's presence continually and was eaten by the priests when it was a week old. With bread it could be done. But not with grape juice. Natural airborne yeast begins to ferment the juice almost immediately after it is expressed from the grape.

Wine Offered to Jesus at the Crucifixion

When Jesus was crucified he was offered wine mixed with gall or myrrh. The Bible says that he refused it (Matt. 27:34; Mark 15:23). This drink should not, however, be confused with the wine vinegar that he accepted later on (Matt. 27:48).

Gall or myrrh was a narcotic used as a painkiller by the ancients. By mingling it with wine, it would be even more effective. This drink, called by the Romans *sopor,* was regularly offered to the condemned just before their crucifixion. It was provided by an association of wealthy women in Jerusalem who prepared it for that purpose.[9]

Jesus knew what it was and refused it. He had come to taste to the full the horror of human death.

Later, when he was thirsty, he did accept some wine vinegar in a sponge. This was probably *homez,* a low-alcohol mix of water and the dregs of the wine vat. The lesson we learn about wine from Jesus is not abstinence. It is moderation.

---

9. James Hastings (ed.), A *Dictionary of Christ and the Gospels*, vol. 2, p. 212.

8

Wine in the New Testament Church

Did believers in the New Testament church drink wine? The thought is anathema to many Christians. Yet, if we are to be faithful to Scripture, we must let the record speak for itself. We shall examine the following evidence:

1. *The Question of Drunkenness on Pentecost* (Acts 2:13)
2. *Abuse of Wine at Corinth* (1 Cor. 11:20–21)
3. *Paul on Temperance and Moderation* (Gal. 5:22–23; Phil. 4:5; Titus 1:7–8; 2:2–3)
4. *Church Leaders Not to Indulge in "Much Wine"* (1 Tim. 3:2–3, 8)

The Question of Drunkenness on Pentecost

On Pentecost the disciples, filled with the Holy Spirit, proclaimed the gospel in foreign tongues to the worshipers gathered in Jerusalem from many lands. Some in the crowd were amazed; others were perplexed. But one group ridiculed what they saw, saying, "They have had too much wine" (Acts 2:13). The important word in this passage is "wine," a translation of the Greek word *gleukos*, sometimes translated "new wine."

The meaning of this word is important to the legalistic prohibitionist because he argues that "new wine," or *gleukos*, is unfermented and was the wine used by believers in those days. He says the accusation that the disciples were drunk on *gleukos* should be dismissed as "mockery run wild" because the mockers are really saying, "These abstainers are drunk on grape juice."[1]

Peter Takes Them Seriously

Peter's response leads me to a different conclusion, however. He says,

> "Fellow Jews and all of you who are in Jerusalem, let me explain this to you; listen carefully to what I say. These men are not drunk, as you suppose. It's only nine in the morning!" [Acts 2:14].

He then goes on to explain Joel's prophecy about the "day of the Lord" (cf. Joel 2:28–32). Peter knows that these onlookers are not jesting. They really believe that the disciples are drunk. So he meets their legitimate accusation with a legitimate answer: "It's only nine in the morning!"

The Jews ate only bread in the morning—about ten, after the morning sacrifice. Meat was the fare for the evening meal, the main meal of the day. They drank wine only when they ate meat, which would have been in the evening. According to Ecclesiastes, it is only godless "princes" who eat in the morning, especially with wine in order to get drunk. The godly eat in due season (Eccles. 10:16–17).[2]

Certainly Peter would not have dignified mockery or jest with an explanation. That kind of person is simply ignored.

Was "New Wine" Intoxicating?

This passage raises the legitimate question of whether "new wine" was intoxicating. Indeed it was! Since the grape harvest was some four

---

1. Jack Van Impe, *Alcohol: The Beloved Enemy*, p. 132.

2. R. C. H. Lenski, *The Interpretation of The Acts of the Apostles*, p. 72.

to eight months past, no fresh grape juice was available. By this time the must from the most recent vintage, the "new wine," would have aerobically fermented enough to have a fairly high alcohol content. Even if the Jews followed the procedure of "bottling" the wine and immersing it in water for thirty days, they would not have had grape juice but young, sweet, fermented wine that had undergone some anaerobic ferment. In chapter 4 we saw that *aigleukos* ("always *gleukos*") or *semper mustum* ("always must") was *not* grape juice. It was "must," the juice of the grape in aerobic ferment, a process that began almost immediately in the wine vat.

Peter does not deny the possibility of *gleukos* producing drunkenness, because it could. His argument, therefore, takes a different direction. He gives a serious answer to a legitimate question. It is not wine but the Holy Spirit.

Abuse of Wine at Corinth

Another passage that has to do with wine in the New Testament church is in 1 Corinthians 11. The Corinthians were known as a carnal lot. It is no surprise, then, that some prohibitionists would accuse them of abusing the ordinance of communion by getting drunk. And from what Paul says it does sound as though this is the case: "When you come together, it is not the Lord's Supper you eat, for as you eat, each of you goes ahead without waiting for anybody else. One remains hungry, another gets drunk" (1 Cor. 11:20–21).

According to the prohibitionist view, the Corinthians were using wine rather than grape juice without apostolic approval. They say that Paul attempted to correct this by reminding them of the original feast in the Upper Room, where—so they claim—wine was not used. This is why, according to the prohibitionist view, the word *wine* is not used by Paul (1 Cor. 11:23–26).[3]

What Was the Abuse?

It is true that the situation got so bad that God executed the death penalty on the offenders (1 Cor. 11:29–32). But I do not agree with the

3. Van Impe, *Alcohol*, p. 133.

reason why it was done—that they were getting drunk at the Lord's Table. The abuse was not drunkenness nor the fact they drank wine. The problem was that their spirit or attitude was wrong.

Communion in those days was not celebrated as it is today, with a morsel of bread and a little cup of grape juice. It was a love feast where the communicants had a meal together, just as they did in the Upper Room. The feast was closed with the memorial service that we call communion.

The problem in Corinth was that some believers took this opportunity to impress others with their wealth. They brought sumptuous dishes to the feast. And, as if their prideful attitude were not bad enough, they would not share their meal with those who had little or nothing to bring. They would eat their own dinner while others went hungry. Paul rebuked them for this:

> Don't you have homes to eat and drink in? Or do you despise the church of God and humiliate those who have nothing? What shall I say to you? Shall I praise you for this? Certainly not! [1 Cor. 11:22].

The purpose of the feast was not to impress others. If we want to impress people, we should do it at home. The wealthy Corinthians were guilty of humiliating the have-nots.

Did the Corinthians Get Drunk?

Did the Corinthians get drunk at the Lord's Table? I don't think they did. The word translated "drunk" in verse 21 is *methuo*, which can mean anything from satiation to gross intoxication. Paul is not chiding them for gross intoxication. They most likely were full of food and cheerfully sated with wine.

If they were drunk, I doubt Paul would have treated them gently. He never treated the Corinthians gently on other issues. If drinking wine were a sin and these people were drunk at the Lord's Table, Paul would have been quite blunt. He would have let them know that both their use and abuse of alcohol were sinful. But he broaches neither subject. His quarrel with them is that they did not share their meal!

In this context Paul reminds the Corinthians of the institution of the ordinance at the first love feast. At that feast there was a sense of

community and solemnity. At the Corinthian communion table os-
tentation and gaiety were displayed. They are condemned not for what
they ate and drank, but for the manner in which they did it. It was
unworthy of the meaning and solemnity of the occasion:

> Therefore, whoever eats the bread or drinks the cup of the Lord in an
> unworthy manner will be guilty of sinning against the body and blood
> of the Lord. A man ought to examine himself before he eats of the
> bread and drinks of the cup [1 Cor. 11:27–28].

Paul says that their attitude, not their food or drink, was the problem.
This was supposed to be a solemn occasion, but the well-heeled
Corinthians used it as an occasion to impress others. It was an occasion that was to celebrate the communion of the saints, but the
wealthy wouldn't even share their meal!

Paul's summary statement conclusively supports this interpretation:

> So then, my brothers, when you come together to eat, wait for each
> other. If anyone is hungry, he should eat at home, so that when you
> meet together it may not result in judgment . . . [1 Cor. 11:33–34].

If Paul had wanted to castigate the Corinthians for something as
serious as the prohibitionist alleges, he certainly would have been
more direct than he was, and his summary statement would have
stated clearly that they were to stop drinking wine and go back to
grape juice.

Paul on Temperance and Moderation

Other evidence of the use of wine in the New Testament church is
found in passages in which Paul urges temperance and moderation.
This suggests that he allowed the limited use of alcoholic beverages.

But the legalistic prohibitionist says that Paul did no such thing,
that even though we are commanded to eat and drink to the glory of
God (1 Cor. 10:31),

there is not a hint that this drinking involves beverage alcohol. Disobedience does not bring glory to God. One can only act to the glory of God when his action is within the framework of biblical revelation.

We have already seen that intoxicating wine is presented in the Bible as an enemy, a mocker, a producer of poverty, and a symbol of divine wrath. Therefore, it is inconceivable that Paul would urge his readers to use this destructive substance in the hope of bringing glory to God.[4]

We are back to the legalism-liberty debate. The legalist declares sin what the Bible does not declare sin. He does not understand that the Bible says the *abuse* of alcohol is sin, not its *use*. The use of alcohol is a "disputable matter" and therefore a matter of liberty (Rom. 14:1).

Paul, the great champion of liberty, understood this difference. His urging us to moderation and temperance is the kind of caution given us in the Old Testament. This warning is found in such statements as, "Every man that strives for mastery is temperate in all things . . ." (1 Cor. 9:25, KJV). The "all things" has reference to that which is not sin. Sin, of course, is to be avoided.

Paul urges temperance and moderation in other passages:

The fruit of the Spirit includes temperance (Gal. 5:22–23)

Our moderation is to be demonstrated to all men (Phil. 4:5)

The elder must be temperate (Titus 1:7–8)

Aged people are to be temperate (Titus 2:2–3).

"Temperance" is a very good word and was used down to the twentieth century in its proper sense—moderation. The early "temperance" societies in America did not advocate total abstinence. They allowed the temperate or moderate use of alcohol, particularly beer and wine, though they did call for the avoidance of distilled spirits. It was not until the early twentieth century that "temperance" came to mean "total abstinence."

---

4. Ibid., p. 136.

Church Leaders Not to Indulge in "Much Wine"

A final line of evidence that wine was used in the New Testament church is the instruction Paul gives to overseers (elders) and deacons in the Pastoral Epistles. There they are told not to indulge in much wine:

> Now the overseer must be above reproach, the husband of but one wife, temperate, self-controlled, respectable, hospitable, able to teach, not given to much wine, not violent but gentle, not quarrelsome, not a lover of money. . . . Deacons, likewise, are to be men worthy of respect, sincere, not indulging in much wine, and not pursuing dishonest gain [1 Tim. 3:2–3, 8].

Does Paul suggest that the elders and deacons may use wine so long as they don't overdo? The legalist says that this is not the implication at all. He says that Paul does not allow *some* wine any more than *some* gossip or *some* greed.[5]

Legalists cannot seem to see that they again are declaring sin what God does not declare sin. Of course Paul could not allow for *some* gossip or greed, since those behaviors are sin. He can allow for *some* wine, however, because sin is in the abuse of wine, not in its use. This is why the apostle must say that they are not to be "given to much wine" or "indulging in much wine." It is the amount, not the act itself, that is the issue here.

Another possible interpretation is that the elders are prohibited not from drinking wine but from being in the company of those who do. The words translated "given to much wine" are from a Greek word meaning "beside wine" (*paroinos*), which was descriptive of those who got drunk at drinking bouts.[6]

This may be the meaning, but I don't think so. It is true that the Corinthians were instructed not to fellowship with a brother who was immoral or disorderly (1 Cor. 5:11). But that was a matter of church discipline. It is difficult to believe that a Christian should stay away

---

5. Ibid., p. 137.

6. Robert Teachout, "The Use of 'Wine' in the Old Testament," p. 442.

from *anyone* who gets drunk. The example of Jesus as the friend of sinners and the rapport he had with them argue against this kind of separatistic thinking.

The warnings to the elder or overseer are to be understood in their historical context. The leaders of the Jewish community, such as the Scribes and Pharisees, and the officers of Rome's army of occupation set an example of leadership that the church leaders might be tempted to follow. They were not respectable, self-controlled people but were violent in their ways. They used slapping as a badge of authority. This is why the Jewish believers in the Gospels were told to "turn the other cheek." We saw this kind of authoritarianism at Jesus' trial, where he was slapped. Those leaders were also quarrelsome and lovers of money. Officials in that day commonly took bribes. They were also known for infidelity and drunkenness. The leaders of God's church were not to be like this.

Though temperance in all things, including wine, was binding on all Christians, it was especially important to warn the leaders of the New Testament church not to pattern their behavior after the Jewish and Roman officials.

Christians are never at liberty to abuse alcohol. To do so is to sin. But they are at liberty to use it in moderation. How and where they do use it is governed by the laws of love and responsibility, which are at the heart of Christian liberty.

9

When Someone You Love Drinks Too Much

Though the Bible permits Christians to drink, with the stipulation that we do not let it damage ourselves or others, we may have some difficulty deciding how much is too much. State laws put an outside limit on the "too much" criterion when they charge a person with intoxication if his blood alcohol content (BAC) is .05 or above. But this does not begin to address the issue.

How Much Is Too Much?

Whether that person you love drinks two beers or eight martinis, drinks every day, or gets drunk occasionally, he is drinking too much if drinking interferes with the normal activities of his life. (As previously noted, throughout this book I have employed standard usage—the indefinite masculine pronoun. The drinker may, however, be a she.) It is too much when alcohol becomes the most important thing in the life of the drinker. It is too much when you feel that you must cover up for the drinker, or when the drinker answers every plea to stop drinking with: "I'm not an alcoholic; I can stop drinking when I want." The drinker may even stop drinking for a day or a week or more to "prove" that alcohol can be controlled.[1]

That person you love is drinking too much when:

1. You worry about how much he drinks.
2. You have money problems because of his drinking.
3. You tell lies to cover up his drinking.
4. You feel that his drinking is more important than you.
5. You believe the drinker's behavior is caused by his companions.
6. Meal times are delayed frequently because of the drinker.
7. You make threats to leave if he doesn't stop drinking.
8. You kiss the drinker hello to try to smell his breath.
9. You're afraid to upset him because it may set off a drinking bout.
10. You have been hurt or embarrassed by the drinker's behavior.
11. Every holiday seems to be spoiled by drinking.
12. You have considered calling the police because of his drinking behavior.
13. You find yourself searching for hidden liquor.
14. You think that if the drinker loved you he would stop drinking to please you.
15. You have refused social invitations out of fear you'd be embarrassed.
16. You sometimes feel guilty when you think of the methods you have employed to control the drinker.
17. You think that if the drinker stopped drinking your other problems would be solved.
18. You try to scare the drinker into saying he's sorry by threatening to hurt yourself.
19. Others find you hard to get along with because you are so angry over his drinking.
20. You feel that no one understands your problem.[2]

---

1. "My Wife Drinks Too Much," Al-Anon Family Groups, p. 7.
2. "Al-Anon: Is It for You?" Al-Anon Family Groups, pp. 1–2.

If three or more of the above are characteristic of your situation, your loved one is using alcohol to excess.

But what do you do about it? Your first reaction may be to reason with the drinker to get him to see the damage or the potential danger of his behavior. The Bible may be employed to add weight to the argument.

The Alcoholic and Problem Drinker

You will be frustrated to find that the alcoholic and problem drinker (they are not the same) do not respond to moral arguments because the problem goes beyond their own ability to cope. The "alcoholic" has a physiological susceptibility to addiction and over time develops an addiction to alcohol. Acetaldehyde, the intermediate byproduct of alcohol metabolism, appears to be a major villain.[3] The alcoholic needs medical attention! The basic problem loved ones face is that the alcoholic will not admit his need for help.

The "problem drinker" is not a true alcoholic as defined above, but his irresponsible alcohol use creates problems for himself and others.[4] A recent study suggests that there may be a connection between personality and problem drinking. The particular personalities at risk are those one psychologist' calls "antisocial personalities" (ASPs). These people, once called "sociopaths," tend to be charming, manipulative, attention seeking, rebellious, impulsive, egocentric, and ready abusers of drugs, alcohol, other people, and themselves. They make up 25 percent of the alcohol-consuming population. This is an extraordinary ratio when we consider that ASPs make up only 3 percent of the general population.[5]

ASPs, who tend to be intense people, drink to change or moderate their moods. They have unusually reactive autonomic nervous systems and emotional under-control, which helps explain why they enjoy alcohol more than most people. Alcohol becomes both a seda-

---

3. James R. Milam and Katherine Ketcham, *Under the Influence*, p. 35.

4. Ibid.

5. "Genes, and Personality, and Alcoholism," *Psychology Today* (January 1985): 38.

tive and a stimulant. They use it to hype themselves up or calm themselves down. Their aim is not so much relief of physical craving as it is mood alteration.[6]

The Christian may insist that the answer to the irresponsible drinker's problem is God's Word. After all, is it not quick and powerful and sharper than a two-edged sword? (Heb. 4:12).

But the person who drinks too much must first be convinced that he has a problem! And the reason why so many drinkers are not convinced they have a problem is that their families often use the wrong approach and keep God from dealing directly with the drinker through adversity. A family's first reaction is usually to reason with the drinker to get him to see his sin or the damage caused by his drinking. When that fails, anger and resentment goad them to complain or threaten.

My advice in one word is DON'T. If you are to be successful in dealing with the drinker, whether he is on his way to alcoholism or is a problem drinker, the first lesson you must learn is that you cannot change *him*, but you can change *yourself.* By changing yourself you will put the drinker in the very best position to see that drinking is *his* problem and only *he* can decide to do something about it.

In this chapter we shall consider how concerned family and friends can change themselves and avoid enabling the drinker to continue his destructive drinking habit. They can do this by refusing to make the drinking problem their problem and by refusing to take the responsibility either to get the loved one to stop his drinking or to bail him out of the mess he creates for himself.

Though I will deal with the adult and adolescent drinker in separate chapters, there are many areas where family and friends need to employ the same strategy with both. But because the adolescent is a minor and is, by drinking *any amount*, violating the law—and because society expects parents to meet the dependency needs of the minor—the adolescent drinker presents a special set of problems.

This does not mean that dependency is not a problem with the adult drinker. Quite the contrary. The adult's dependency on others to

---

6. Ibid., p. 44.

keep him fed, clothed, and employed, and his denial of that dependency, is one of the major problems that family and friends must learn to deal with. Indeed, the alcoholic and the problem drinker, whether adolescent or adult, learn to behave as little gods who coerce or manipulate a cast of characters to support their excessive drinking.

The Drinker and His Supporting Cast

Excessive drinking, whether by the alcoholic or the problem drinker, involves the drinker and usually at least three members of a supporting cast whom he controls. He drinks irresponsibly and gets others to react to his drinking and its consequences. The drinker then responds negatively to their reaction and drinks again, which sets in motion the merry-go-round of blame and denial.[7]

The Drinker

The drinker in question has learned that drinking makes him feel better. For a few hours he is relieved of anxiety and tension, his loneliness is dispelled, and his problems seem insignificant. Because of the profound relief he experiences, he looks at alcohol as a blessing. And because of this he will not accept the judgment of others that it is a curse. He will ignore criticism, shift blame, and/or deny even the most obvious evidence of the damage his drinking is doing—because those hours under the influence are a welcome escape for him.

There is another reality the drinker chooses to ignore, deny, or explain away. And that is his dependency. Though he may appear smart and successful on the surface, he really depends on others to keep him fed, clothed, and employed while he continues his irresponsible and destructive drinking. He never will admit this, however. He manages to get others to meet his dependency needs by ignoring or denying that he has any part in his misfortunes. To hear him tell it, he is the victim of people or circumstances. And, as a victim, he maintains that he has a perfect right to expect his family and friends to come to his aid.

---

7. "Alcoholism: A Merry-Go-Round Named Denial," Al-Anon Family Groups.

Another denial is the amount he drinks. Not only does the problem drinker *need* a drink, which he denies is a sign of his growing addiction or dependence, he also conceals the amount he drinks. It is his way of trying to keep others from seeing the large place that alcohol has in his life. He drinks because he craves it or feels the need to alter his mood, and he drinks a great deal not simply to reach a state of intoxication but also to guarantee that the state of blissful escape will last for some time. He may secretly drink all day, day in and day out, to the point where he is never really sober. The result is that his friends cannot tell that he is drunk either, because he stays that way most of the time. But if faced with the realities of his drinking, he will angrily deny it. *There is no reasoning with the alcoholic or problem drinker.* You will not solve your problem with them by reasoning. It is only when things finally reach a critical point and they are permitted to face that crisis without being bailed out that they are in the best position to come to terms with their drinking.

Excessive drinking eventually leads to trouble. Though there are many different ways in which this can happen—chronic absenteeism that threatens his job, DWI (Driving While Intoxicated) arrest, or even vehicular homicide—he is a dependent person who has been able, when under the influence of alcohol, to delude himself into thinking he is independent. And yet, by continuing his drinking, he makes even more of a mess of his life, which in turn makes him even more dependent on others. When he finds himself in real trouble as a result of his drinking, he will try to ignore it, confident that someone will bail him out without his asking—which perpetuates the illusion of independence. He reasons that after all, he didn't *ask* for help. Or, if no one steps in, he may angrily demand help from family and friends, reminding them that it is the reasonable duty of loving people. But all the while he is ignoring the problem or demanding that others bail him out, he is denying that he is responsible for the mess he got into. It is always someone else's fault or there is some reason beyond his control for circumstances working against him. Though dependent and irresponsible, he will not face it.

Even alcoholics and problem drinkers who readily admit that they were wrong and need help will often, after the trouble has blown over, deny that anything bad really happened or in some way will minimize or excuse their behavior. They will return to their drinking patterns, confident that they can get away with it again because someone will always be there to pick up the pieces. This has the effect of perpetuating their dependency on the supporting cast of family and friends who, in the name of love—albeit, misguided love—will bail them out again and again.

The Enabler

The alcoholic and problem drinker have among their supporting cast of characters one or more Enablers. This is the helpful soul who feels compelled to save the drinker from his immediate crisis and defuse the terrible tension created by drinking.

Though the Enabler's intentions are as pure as the driven snow, he or she is blind to the manipulation of the drinker. Enablers cannot see that by always being there to bail out the drinker, they perpetuate the drinker's dependency on them and rob the drinker of the motivation and skills needed to solve his own problems. An Enabler takes away the drinker's motivation by never permitting him to suffer the consequences of his drinking. Enablers never let the drinker develop his own skills in coping with alcohol. These skills are not needed, as far as the drinker is concerned, because the Enabler will bail him out.

We sometimes see this pattern in a marriage where the do-gooder is a wife who needs to keep her husband dependent on her so she can play nurse or martyr and have the admiration of friends who say, "You're a remarkable woman to put up with a husband like that!" In this kind of marriage it is not unusual, when the husband finds the path to sobriety, for the woman to divorce him and marry another alcoholic or irresponsible man whom she can care for to the applause of others.

Sometimes the Enabler-Wife perpetuates her husband's dependency simply out of a need for her own survival. For example, her husband jeopardizes his job with his drinking. If he wakes up in the morning so hung-over that he cannot go to work, she covers for him by "calling in sick" for him. When asked why she did not leave with him the responsibility to explain himself to the boss, she will say that he might lose his job (financial insecurity for her), and that he would get terribly ugly and abusive (personal insecurity for her). This Enabler really is not acting in her husband's best interest. She is protecting herself. Any marriage partner who wants to show unselfish love for her or his spouse and truly help the other must stop bailing out the errant husband or wife.

This type of Enabler is great at playing the game of "Why don't you . . . ?/Yes, but . . . ." The best minds in the world can come up with suggestions—"Why don't you . . . ?" But the enabling spouse will always have a good reason why she or he can't do any of those things—"Yes, but . . . ." Until these Enablers come to the place of being willing to admit that it is not the spouse's sobriety that is their main concern but their own welfare and safety, they will continue to be Enablers.

The Victim

Another member of the drinker's supporting cast is the Victim. The same person can play the role of both Enabler and Victim, as with the wife above. Rather than be victimized by the consequences of her husband's drinking, she will act as an Enabler. She may at times, however, play the part of Victim. She may weep or plead with her husband until she realizes that he will not take responsibility for his behavior, and then she will switch to the Enabler role to protect herself. Or her husband may top her weeping and pleading with his own weeping and remorse over what he has done and plead for her help. This may be enough to move her from the position of Victim to that of Enabler. At any rate, she cannot see that she is guilty of misguided love.

Sometimes the Victim is an employer who needs the drinker to be productive and often, out of this need and a misguided sense of human kindness, will make allowances, adjustments, and excuses. But in doing so the employer becomes an Enabler and helps the drinker to continue irresponsible drinking without losing his job. The Victim teaches the drinker an important lesson—he can victimize others and get away with it! Not only that, he can turn them around and get them to make his irresponsible drinking possible! When a driver discovers that he can drive under the influence (DUI), drive while intoxicated (DWI), or even commit vehicular homicide while under the influence and get away with no more than a slap on the wrist, he believes that the Victims will accept his irresponsibility and always bail him out by becoming Enablers. It is not unloving or unkind for the Victim, or the court acting on behalf of the Victim, to say to the drinker, "No, we will not accept your behavior. You didn't 'have an accident,' as if it were something you have no responsibility for. What you had was the logical consequence of your behavior—your ignoring your problem and your choice to drive while intoxicated."

The Provoker

Another important member of the supporting cast is the Provoker, sometimes called the Persecutor. "He," though more often "she" (wife or mother), is the person with whom the drinker lives. Such a woman is angry and bitter over the drinker's destructive behavior and the mess he makes of his life, which she has to live with. A great deal of her anger stems from the fact that she tries so hard to keep the marriage or home together, but the drinker continues in his destructive behavior, refuses to cooperate, and thwarts her best efforts to get him to stop drinking.

This Provoker serves a useful function in the supporting cast. She gives the drinker a good reason not to feel guilty about his destructive behavior! He can use the old copout, "You'd drink, too, if you were married to the woman I'm married to," or ". . . had a mother who hassled you all the time."

Provokers learn to adjust to the problem and eventually become Enablers. They find that they cannot talk to their drinking spouse or teenager about the problem. To do so only invites bitter retorts and blame for the problem. They are accused of being unloving and not understanding. So, when a Provoker-Spouse or -Parent doesn't get anywhere, to avoid becoming a Victim, she or he once again becomes an Enabler—and the merry-go-round continues to turn.

Love, Justice, and the Drinker

"Love" is a much-abused word, particularly when it comes to the alcoholic and problem drinker, whose common complaint is, "If you loved me you'd be more understanding and wouldn't hassle me." Love, to these people, hears no evil, sees no evil, and speaks no evil.

Or, if that is impossible because of the magnitude of the evil, love fixes the damage so the drinker can continue the drinking with as few consequences as possible. But this is not love. Love is meaningless unless it is seen in relationship with justice.

Man's sense of justice rises out of instincts created in the image of a God who is just. This is found in all cultures, Christian and otherwise. The aim of justice is to extract the payment of damages from those who are guilty of wrongdoing.

Love does not ignore justice but agrees that its demands must be met. Those who say they love the drinker really do not if they continue to enable his behavior. They fail either by saying that no wrong was done and that justice demands no satisfaction, when in fact wrong *has* been done—or they see that wrong has been done, that justice demands satisfaction, and they themselves decide to satisfy justice.

But only God can do that sort of thing! God is the authority on right and wrong, and when well-meaning spouses or parents try to minimize or cover up wrong behavior and the damage done by the drinker, they are acting like little gods. Or, when they agree that wrong has been done and that justice requires satisfaction and attempt to satisfy justice by paying the penalty themselves—a fine and bail money for DWI, for example—they again are playing God. *Only God can satisfy justice for someone else.* Indeed, this is exactly what God, the Father of Jesus Christ, did when he sent his Son to die for our sins. He loved us enough to satisfy the demands of justice with the sacrifice of his Son.

It is true that the alcoholic and problem drinker behave like little gods when they act as though they can do whatever they wish and will hear no one tell them otherwise. But it is the loved ones of the drinker who really act like gods. *They* decide what is sin and what is not sin. *They* decide when the claims of justice need not be satisfied. Or, if they do decide that wrong has been done and justice must be satisfied, *they* make everything all right. They attempt to atone for the sin themselves! Marvel of marvels—do we now have a fourth person of the Trinity?

I know that Enabler-Victim-Provokers do not *feel* like gods. They feel angry, frustrated, and helpless. They feel scared and see their world caving in because of a loved one's excessive drinking. But as far as the drinker is concerned, the spouse or parent or friend is behaving like a god! The alcohol abuser's sense of self-worth drops yet another notch when this little god either declares that the drinker has not sinned or atones for it with that remarkable ability to cover up or fix things. Indeed, the loved one is so good at it that she or he should have been with God at the fall of Adam. Perhaps he could have used the advice!

The love that we are called on to exercise toward the alcoholic and problem drinker is a love that acknowledges wrong and allows justice to be satisfied without our doing it. It also cares enough not to behave as if we were little gods and could be the substitutionary sacrifice for the drinker's sins.

The love we are called on to exercise is the love of a fellow sinner and fellow struggler who, refusing to be a little god any longer, suffers *with* the drinker instead *for* him. It means doing practical things, such as not covering bad checks but leaving with him the responsibility of having to answer for what he has done—and suffering the financial penalty with him. It means not "calling in sick" for him when he's hung over but instead suffering the anxiety with him of wondering if he will lose his job.

When we stop playing God and suffer with the drinker, we make marriage and family life possible because we have thereby joined the human race. We no longer are up in the heavens, far above with our self-anointed divine powers. We are fellow-sufferers and fellow-strugglers with the sinner. That's what marriage and family is all about.

It may be that you will discover that you cannot take the suffering and must separate or divorce to preserve your own life and sanity. That is an individual matter, and only you can decide. In the meantime, if you truly want to help, *lovingly detach yourself.* You detach yourself by refusing to act like a god, and you do it lovingly by suffering the consequences of the drinker's irresponsibility as best you can. Al-Anon says this about detachment:

Detachment is neither kind nor unkind. It does not imply evaluation of the person or situation from which we are detaching. It is simply a means for us to recover from the adverse effects on our lives of living with someone afflicted with the disease of alcoholism. Detachment helps families look at their situations realistically and objectively, thereby making intelligent decisions possible.

If you think that the loved one you are concerned about may be drinking too much, you may find help in Al-Anon. People in Al-Anon learn the following:

Not to suffer because of the actions or reactions of other people.

Not to allow ourselves to be used or abused in the interest of another's recovery.

Not to do for others what they should do for themselves.

Not to manipulate situations so others will eat, go to bed, get up, or pay bills.

Not to cover up for another's mistakes or misdeeds.

Not to create a crisis.

Not to prevent a crisis if it is in the natural course of events.[8]

Though it may be scary to think about detaching, and even though things may get worse before they get better, once the alcoholic and problem drinker realize that "the fourth person of the Trinity" no longer is going to atone for their sin, they will be given the very best opportunity to come to terms with their drinking.

Al-Anon Support

Taking this course of action is terribly difficult to do without help. And constructive help is found in Al-Anon, a support group of people who themselves know what it means to leave the pantheon of the gods and become mortals who suffer along with the alcoholic and problem drinker. Al-Anon is a separate fellowship from Alcoholics Anonymous (AA). It attempts to meet the needs of those whose lives are affected by someone else's drinking. Like AA, Al-Anon stresses the anonymity of its members.

---

8. "Detachment," Al-Anon Family Groups.

Al-Anon is supported by voluntary contributions of its members. The money goes for the expenses of weekly meeting places and for the maintenance of service centers.

For Al-Anon meetings near you, consult your phone directory. If none is listed, write the headquarters at P.O. Box 182, Madison Square Station, New York, NY 10159.

Not only is the decision to drink a matter of personal choice under liberty, the individual who drinks excessively and abuses alcohol also is the one who must make the decision to stop! We will examine this thesis in the next chapter.

10

Can We Make Them Quit?

The philosophy of Alcoholics Anonymous states clearly that the alcoholic cannot be protected from the bottle or the consequences of his drinking. This conviction is stated again and again in AA literature:

> A frequent mistake is to attempt to protect the alcoholic from alcohol by bending every effort to keep him away from the bottle and the bottle away from him. This cannot be achieved short of incarceration or commitment and even under these circumstances some manage to find alcohol. It is hard for the family to learn not to try to prevent the drinking, but any battle they win today over the bottle will be fought again tomorrow. Winning the war against the overall illness is the objective. Motivating the alcoholic to have a desire to stop drinking and to accept help in this effort is far more effective than trying to take the bottle away. The only way this motivation can be accomplished is by allowing the drinking and all its consequences to become so painful in itself that the alcoholic will seek escape from the intolerable pain caused by drinking. This means offering the alcoholic love and understanding in his sobriety, but not protecting him from the bottle or the consequences of drinking.[1]

1. "A Guide for the Family of the Alcoholic," Al-Anon Family Groups.

In spite of this successful, time-tested philosophy, health professionals have in recent years begun to advocate a different approach—"confrontational strategy." Their favorite word is "intervention."

The idea of confrontational strategy is to bring family pressure to bear on the alcoholic to force him into treatment. The examples of Betty Ford and Elizabeth Taylor, both of whom responded to pressure by their families, often are offered. One psychologist writes,

> The widely accepted belief that alcoholics have to "hit bottom" before they can be helped has been completely discredited in recent years . . . . Well over half of the alcoholics now being treated successfully were forced into treatment against their wills; they did not want to stop drinking, but certain crises in their lives backed them into a corner and forced them to seek help.[2]

I cannot be so optimistic. Alcoholics forced into treatment are not going to respond unless they are ready. If they are not, they will play the usual alcoholic game of pretending to go along with family pressure, knowing all the while that they will go back to the bottle. Those who do respond to confrontation do so not because of outside pressure but in spite of it. AA has proved over the years that an alcoholic will not stop drinking until he is ready.

This does not mean that the medical community advocating confrontation completely discounts AA. In fact, it may even adopt some of AA's techniques—or at least sound as though it does. For example, it sounds as though they are following an AA principle when they advocate that family and friends develop an emotional detachment from the user or abuser and that AA be used for long-term sobriety.[3] But their writing reveals that the AA principle of detachment is not fully understood. Indeed, the new thinking about alcohol and drug abuse and dependency is flawed in three areas.

Hitting Bottom

The confrontationalists' thinking is flawed in the first place, in their belief that an alcoholic can be made to quit drinking. This stands in

---

2. James R. Milam and Katherine Ketcham, *Under the Influence*, pp. 118–19.

3. Ibid., pp. 120–22.

stark contrast to the major tenet of AA that a person other than the alcoholic himself cannot make him quit. The decision to quit must come from the alcoholic. This is sound reasoning and is a tried and true principle. Attempts to force the alcoholic to quit with threats and tearful scenes—or even reasonable conversation—lead to nothing but defensiveness, denial, or promises that are never fulfilled. The only thing the alcohol abuser understands is consequences. And he must experience these effects as consequences that he has brought upon himself by his alcohol abuse.

Though exponents of confrontation may point to some success stories where families have forced the alcohol abuser into treatment, I am not sure that the abuser entered treatment because of the confrontation. Had he not been willing to give up his alcohol abuse, he either would have been unresponsive to the confrontation or he may have even used the treatment to get his family and friends off his back.

The abuser may promise to get treatment and even enter treatment as the price he has to pay to get people to stop hassling him. In time he figures it will all blow over and he can go back to the bottle.

Emotional Detachment

A second area in which confrontational thinking is flawed is in its misunderstanding of detachment. Those who hold this inaccurate view of detachment don't go far enough with it.

In the AA program helping alcoholics come to terms with their alcoholism is achieved through emotional detachment by nondrinking family and friends. The new "intervention" thinkers do not understand that emotional detachment by family and friends creates the environment necessary for an alcohol abuser to hit bottom and decide on his own that he must do something about the problem.

"Detachment" to the new thinkers does not go that far. It simply means not becoming emotionally embroiled in the abuser's excuses and denials or not believing that they are somehow responsible for causing his unhappiness.[4]

---

4. Ibid., pp. 120–121.

This is fine, but only up to a point. It ignores the place of detachment in AA philosophy that is essential in keeping us from being Enablers. Detachment means not only avoiding guilt trips when the abuser plays Victim or Persecutor. It also means that family and friends refuse to clean up the mess that the abuser makes of his life. Basic to the AA approach is the philosophy that we cannot make ourselves happy by controlling the alcoholic's drinking. Indeed, we are unable to do it. We must let go and put that person in the hands of God. But we can control our own lives. We can determine by God's guidance and help what *we* will or will not do. We may not be able to control the abuser's alcohol dependency, but we may decide that we will not permit our own lives to be destroyed by his behavior. And we do this with detachment. We lovingly disengage, giving a message to the abuser: "I love you. But I can't do anything about what you're doing with your life."

The abuser soon finds out that family and friends are not there to clean up the mess he makes of his life. Then he must face the consequences. And it is when the abuser repeatedly and consistently faces the consequences of his behavior because of the disengagement of family and friends that he is in the best position to decide on his own that he needs help.

How this applies to youth, who should be under the control of their parents, I will address in chapter 11. But this much I will say here. Parents have a responsibility to control their children. And the children's immaturity and dependence makes them more amenable to control than adults who have become worldly-wise manipulators. But when all is said and done, when all reasonable attempts to bring children under control fail, the parent may be forced to disengage and exercise "tough love," which essentially abandons the child to the consequences of his behavior.

If the purpose of confrontation by the family is to serve notice on the abuser that they cannot control his life and therefore are going to lovingly detach, that's all right. But it must be clear that they are not trying to control the abuser's life by forcing him into treatment. What they are doing is assuming control of their own lives by detaching.

If the purpose of the confrontation is to coerce the abuser into entering a treatment program, we ignore a fundamental teaching of

AA and assume the role of Provoker or Persecutor. It matters not that our intentions are good. We still set ourselves up for failure by taking this approach and invite the abuser to counter our move by playing the role of Victim.

The abuser, playing Victim, will angrily bluster or tearfully wail that his family doesn't understand him. He maintains that if they did, they wouldn't be confronting him like this. No matter that the family is confronting lovingly and in a spirit of good will. The abuser can throw the session into a tailspin by crazy-making—communication sabotage. He redefines the context of the session as one of ill will in which he is being persecuted by those around him.

It is also possible that he may use a different approach. He may play the Victim with more guile and agree to enter a program without protest. By doing this he is able to keep his family in the role of Enablers, albeit in the name of giving the abuser help for his problem.

In this case, the drinker does not identify his family as Persecutors. Now it is they who run the program or are in treatment with him who are accused of persecuting and victimizing him. He lies when he tells his family that he wants help. And he lies when he leaves the program, claiming that he cannot stand the shabby treatment he is getting there.

Once out of the program, he is able to go back to alcohol, candidly admitting that he has a problem but that his problem is beyond help. This may continue until the family finds another program and coerces him once more to become involved—and the merry-go-round starts all over again.

The Economics of the Problem

This brings us to a third area of conflict between traditional and modern thinking about alcohol abuse—the economics of the problem.

Traditionally, the alcoholic who wanted help went to AA meetings, where he found a support group that could understand him, a sponsor who could be called on for support and encouragement between meetings, and a program of twelve steps that he was required to work out. He began the program by taking the first step—admitting that he was powerless over alcohol and that his life had become unmanageable.

Al-Anon, mentioned in the last chapter, was founded in 1954 as an educational program and support group for the nondrinking members of the family. Recognizing that alcohol addiction is a *family* problem, Al-Anon has taken steps to educate the family in how to avoid playing into the abuser's hands and provide a support group that helps them accomplish this objective. Members of Al-Anon also have a twelve-step program, the first step being: "We admitted we were powerless over alcohol—that our lives had become unmanagable."

Another program, Alateen, has also been established. Patterned after Al-Anon, it is geared particularly for the teen whose parent abuses alcohol.

Admittedly, starting sobriety in AA is difficult. Only one in eighteen are able to do it.[5] And there is no detoxification facility, medical support, or professional counseling. Modern thinkers on alcoholism, pointing this out, argue for a comprehensive, disciplined program that includes the following:

in-patient medical detoxification;

a 4-week minimum of in-patient care;

educational programs which stress the physical basis of the disease and its role in causing psychological and social symptoms;

intensive nutritional therapy and education;

strong emphasis on AA for long-term sobriety;

thorough follow-up care;

involvement of the family in treatment and follow-up care.[6]

All of this is well and good and in some cases essential, particularly where detoxification and an alcohol-free environment are required. But such programs can be expensive! The AA program, on the other hand, is free.

---

5. Ibid., p. 132.
6. Ibid., pp. 121–22.

Raising the economic issue often brings howls of protest from the professional community. "How can you put a family's purse ahead of the well-being of one of its members?" I am sometimes asked. This question disturbs me because it reveals an insensitivity toward a family already feeling guilty. It also reveals an unwillingness to look at the economics of the problem.

In answer to that question—putting the purse ahead of the well-being of a family member—my experience with American families is that they are a self-sacrificing lot. In fact, I think sometimes they are too self-sacrificing, which can give the alcoholic the idea that the family has no needs and that the alcoholic's needs always ought to come first.

American families are usually willing to make sacrifices for one of its members if they are sure that the sacrifice is going to bring the desired results. Our citizenry has become much more sophisticated about health care in recent years. We used to place blind trust in doctors, believing that throwing more money at a problem would solve it. Most of us are no longer so naive, and we have become increasingly suspicious of and cynical toward the professional community as a whole.

Americans are also much better educated than they used to be. There is no longer the professional man and the common man. Many "commoners" are well informed about the professions, including the medical profession. They are aware of abuses by the profession and have discovered that more money does not always mean a better solution. Growing tired of the ever-increasing cost of medical care, they are beginning to shop around and look for alternatives to the more expensive solution.

Finding that alternative is not so easy, however. A mind-boggling plethora of institutions and individual counselors offer help to families in need. (See Appendix C for a list of resources.)

But what does a family do with the adolescent drinker? Read on and discover how this special problem can be licked.

11

What to Do with the Adolescent Drinker

Only a few years ago marijuana was the drug of choice among adolescents. Reams of literature were written about it. Parents were taught to know what it looks like, what it smells like, and what symptoms their kids were likely to show if they used it.

Though it is still being used, marijuana is becoming passé. Alcohol, which never did lose its appeal to teens, once again is the drug of choice. Its major appeal is that it is easier to obtain than any other drug.

Christian liberty may permit adults to drink, but adolescents *by law* may not drink. The adolescent who drinks any amount of alcohol is breaking the law, and adults who abet this drinking are also guilty.

The emphasis of this chapter is not on the adolescent who experiments with alcohol—who may try it once or twice, or may even, with great regret, get drunk. A disciplined yet loving household is able to cope with lapses such as this with standard disciplinary procedures:

1. The teen understands that house rules forbid his drinking—even one beer.

2. He understands that violation of this rule will result in discipline.
3. House rules forbid him to ride in a car when the driver has been drinking. If he is stranded without transportation because of this, he may call home for a ride at any time without penalty.
4. If the teenager drives, he understands he will lose his driving privileges for a substantial period of time if he drinks and drives. Even if he owns his car, the rule still applies. Minors must understand that driving is a privilege not a right, and one given only with parental permission. If he has been drinking, he may call home for a ride without losing his car privileges.

The no-penalty rule encourages the teenager to "not take a chance." The parent can expect, however, that the adolescent may not want to reveal the fact that he has been drinking and may still drive under the influence of alcohol. But when he is nailed for breaking this rule, he may be more disposed to ask for a ride the next time!

The parent may ask, "But won't this encourage him to drink? After all, he doesn't lose his car privileges as long as he calls for a ride." Even though car privileges are not lost, this rule encourages safety, while at the same time permitting the parent to monitor the teen's experience with alcohol. When, in parental judgment, the drinking has gone beyond experimentation, the issue is no longer drinking-and-driving but drinking itself, which is prohibited by law and by parental decree.

The parent should say to the teen, "Over the past few months I've become increasingly alarmed over what seems to be more than experimentation with alcohol. Even though it's against the law and a violation of house rules for you to drink, it is becoming a frequent occurrence, and something must be done about it." The teen should then be grounded because of violation of the drinking rule, which effectively keeps him out of the car at the same time. The parent who is both loving and firm will ultimately succeed with a teen who is basically compliant.

I don't worry about this family. The family I worry about is the one that must cope with a teen who is determined to drink and violate any other house rule he feels like violating. This becomes a particularly bad situation when the parents are overwhelmed with other problems, are unable to work together, or the parent is single—particularly a single mother—and must handle this teenager alone. These parents need to know about TOUGHLOVE.

The TOUGHLOVE Movement

Because society expects parents to meet the dependency needs of a minor, parents find it difficult to employ the principles of Al-Anon and thus avoid being Enablers, Victims, or Provokers. Indeed, the incorrigible teenager tells his parents that they are responsible for his care no matter what he does. And the courts, reluctant to intrude into family matters, usually will not intervene unless the teen is drunk and disorderly in public. Even then he is usually remanded to the custody of his parents, and the problem continues.

As with the adult drinker, dependency is the core issue. The adolescent drinker does as his adult counterpart: he denies dependency, though he is essentially dependent on family and friends for the basic necessities of life, and he relies on their taking the responsibility for reducing the consequences of his drinking.

One of the most effective programs for problem adolescents is the TOUGHLOVE movement founded by Phyllis and David York, who themselves had to come to terms with an incorrigible daughter who finally was jailed for armed robbery. The only reason I mention this is to encourage fainthearted parents. The advice the Yorks give has been tested in the crucible of personal experience. Only *after* they decided they would get tough and refuse to bail their daughter out of jail and did not deal directly with her for seven months did they begin to get results. They put it this way:

. . . TOUGHLOVE is loving. TOUGHLOVE is not nasty or abusive or vindictive. TOUGHLOVE means standing firm, knowing what plan to follow to deal with your kid's destructiveness, and loving your child enough to stop acting on wishes, hopes, and fantasies. TOUGHLOVE means loving your child enough to do what has to be done, no matter how hard you find the task.[1]

---

1. Phyllis and David York and Ted Wachtel, *Toughlove*, p. 153.

TOUGHLOVE'S Ten Beliefs

The success of TOUGHLOVE, in part, is found in its "Ten Beliefs"—principles similar to those of Al-Anon. These beliefs are:

1. Family problems have roots and supports in culture.
2. Parents are people too.
3. Parents' material and emotional resources are limited.
4. Parents and kids are not equal.
5. Blaming keeps people helpless.
6. Kids' behavior affects parents; parents' behavior affects kids.
7. Taking a stand precipitates a crisis.
8. From controlled crisis comes positive change.
9. Families need to give and get support in their own community to get change.
10. The essence of family life is cooperation, not togetherness.[2]

Every parent who has an adolescent drinker at home should read the Yorks' book, TOUGHLOVE. In brief, here is the idea of each of the Ten Beliefs, together with my own observations of their applicability to the teen drinker.

Roots in Culture

Incorrigible youths today are not crazy; they are stoned. They don't need "psychologizing" that searches family roots to explain their misbehavior. Indeed, we have been deluded into thinking that if parents will only understand the outrageous teenager, this will somehow correct his bad behavior. But what this actually does is make the teen think that the understanding adult is a pushover and can be victimized.

Our culture is all-too-ready to excuse the outrageous behavior of its kids on the grounds that they come from broken homes or their lives are despairing and meaningless because they are living "under a nuclear shadow." A typical statement comes from The National Council On Alcoholism:

---

2. Ibid., pp. 27–119.

> . . . an adolescent's alcohol abuse is frequently a reaction to and a reflection of existing family dysfunction and that abusive drinking for the adolescent may serve as a means of calling attention to a family situation or crisis so as to provoke the family to recognize and to resolve it.[3]

Kids are excused because so many adults in high places—from the Nixon Presidency down—are rascals at best and criminals at worst. Television, though often unfairly blamed, reflects this attitude with shows like "The Dukes of Hazard," where policemen are boobs, politicians are rascals, and moonshiners are heroes.

The family, as the basic unit of social organization, is also portrayed as impotent and powerless. Situation comedies portray families in chaos and children as the real power in a household. And, unfortunately, this is a somewhat exaggerated reflection of things as they really are!

If parents are powerless and out of control, it is because we accept the blame of teens who tell us that *we* are responsible for their misbehavior. Parents who would help their teen come to terms with his drinking must not take the rap for it. And not only must they refuse to take the blame, they must be careful not to suppose that they have some kind of godlike power to make the teen stop drinking. This does not mean that a parent is powerless to do anything. As with the spouse of the adult alcoholic or problem drinker, parents of a teen drinker must begin by changing themselves. Certainly parents need to be in touch with their teens and understand the pressures on them. But understanding will not get the job done.

Parents Are People Too

Parents are not gods; they are people—mere human beings with foibles and sins just as anyone else. The teen alcohol user and abuser, just as his adult counterpart, needs to keep his parents in the pantheon of gods because it serves two essential needs. It perpetuates the fiction that parents as gods are to meet the dependency needs of their children, and it also gives the teen a marvelous opportunity to

---

3. Ibid., p. 27.

manipulate the parents with guilt when they fail to live up to the teen's expectations. This produces a teen who continually is ungrateful and critical. After all, what would happen if a parent *did* live up to the teenager's expectations? The parent might turn around and expect the teen to live up to *parental* expectations! This attitude also produces parents who are perpetually anxious over the prospect of failing their child and feel guilt-ridden when he does.

Of course, cultural attitudes contribute to the problem. Everywhere parents are being asked if they have done right by their kids. We are asked, for example, "Have you hugged your kid today?" This can be a legitimate question, but not if it implies that not hugging your kid is another evidence of parental failure and is the reason why your kid is an alcoholic or has a problem with drinking or any other area of behavior.

This kind of guilt trip goads parents to spend all their time, energy, and money trying to live up to expectations that God alone can fulfill. And whenever the teen wants an excuse to justify his drinking and outrageous behavior, he can always point to parents who have "failed" him.

Once our kids learn that we are not gods and that we do not intend to be, we break the pattern of manipulative behavior. Remember, it takes two to play a manipulative game—the perpetrator and the victim.

We must not let our culture or our kids maneuver us into the position of playing God. Remember, parents are people too.

Limited Resources

Parents often wonder why their children are greedy and selfish. They wonder if it is something they have done to produce children like this. The fault does not lie with something they have done so much as it is with something they have not done. They have not given their children the message that the family's material and emotional resources are limited and that the children have a responsibility to start carrying some of their own weight.

Our society is obsessed with children and their needs. Designer jeans, wheels to get around on, and a college education are portrayed as inalienable rights of the American teen. All of this is to be dispensed by parents who are supposed to have an endless store of money and patience.

The teen can be taught to respect the parents' material and emotional limits by being given the responsibility to budget his purchases from earnings and allowance—or do without. When the teen must compare the cost of designer jeans with the less-expensive item, he (though it's just as often "she") will decide to go with the lower-priced item. When you refuse to fill up the gas tank in the car for a teen and do not provide money or a credit card for a full tank, the young person either puts gas in the tank, gets a ride with someone else, or stays home.

I quickly learned with my kids never to fill the gas tank. They usually left it empty, hoping I would fill it. So I began leaving it empty too. I would figure out how much gas I needed to get around on a particular day and buy only that much. I also kept a secret stash of gas in a can at home so I could at least get to the gas station if it looked as though the tank was bone dry. As a consequence, the kids kept running out of gas. But they knew better than to call me and ask me to pick them up or bring them gas!

Patience is also a resource that is limited, but it is important that impatience or anger be handled constructively. Deal with it before it reaches explosive proportions. Before you start screaming, sit down with your teen and tell him, "I need to say something. You need not reply if you don't want to, because I'm not going to attack you or ask dumb questions or even try to reason with you. I just want you to know that I feel taken for granted and used and that I'm angry and resentful about it. If you see me backing off and being distant, cool, or cautious, this is the reason why. I'm telling you so you won't have to second-guess what's going on."

Adolescents who use and abuse alcohol expect parents, out of their limitless resources, to enable them to continue their drinking habits. They have learned that they can spend money on alcohol and stay out all night drinking and not attend school regularly or work because their parents will feed them and put gas in the car. If the kid winds up with tickets or faces jail for DWI, good old Mom and Dad will pay the tickets or bail them out.

Parent, make today the first day of a new life for you and your teen. Admit to yourself and your teen that you are not a god and that you have come to the end of your resources. When we as parents stop acting as though our material and emotional resources are limitless, our kids will get the message. Though things may get worse before they get better, you will give them the very best opportunity to come to terms with their drinking or other excessive behavior.

Parents and Kids Are Not Equal

A lot of nonsense has been dispensed by well-meaning professionals over the years about a "democratic family." The child, it was proposed, should have as much a say in family affairs as the parents. After all, the reasoning went, doesn't our Declaration of Independence say that everyone is created equal?

The allusion to our national heritage is inappropriate here. Although our constitution, including its amendments, underscores the right of all citizens to equal protection under the law, many privileges are reserved for those who have reached the age of majority and therefore can be full participants in government by virtue of their right to vote.

With rights go responsibilities, and minors are denied certain rights because they simply are not considered mature enough to handle the responsibilities. They are not allowed to vote because of their immature judgment. They are not allowed to drink alcoholic beverages for the same reason, even though ten million alcoholic adults show themselves incapable of exercising good judgment in this area.

The same philosophy that prescribes withholding certain privileges until a stipulated age also serves to *protect* a minor. For example, parents are held financially responsible for meeting a minor's physical needs until maturity. And a youthful lawbreaker is usually not tried and sentenced under the same judicial procedure as an adult. Such protective safeguards imply that a youth is not fully accountable and responsible until reaching maturity.

The crux of the issue is not the law. It is responsibility. Until the teenager is ready to house, clothe, and feed himself, pay utility bills, and provide his own transportation, including auto and hospital insurance, he better go easy on "rights"—because with rights go responsibilities.

Sometimes when parents respond to a teenager's drinking by imposing restrictions on him, such as no TV or car privileges, they run into the problem of ownership. The teen may own the TV or car. What then? In the case of the TV the parent may say, "It's your TV but our electricity. You will not use our electricity. What is more, if you do and get ugly about it, you will be removed from the bedroom you're using. You may own a TV but you don't own the room. We happen to be paying the mortgage on the house."

In the case of the car, parents usually subsidize a teen's car either by loaning him the money to buy it or letting him be carried on the family's auto-insurance policy. You can let him know that he either leaves the car parked or he will be dropped from your policy and will have to carry his own insurance, which is much more expensive. He also should be told that the Department of Motor Vehicles will be informed if he is an uninsured driver. This should result in his registration being revoked.

It is important, however, to follow the principle that you do not warn of disciplinary action that you cannot or will not enforce. If you are afraid that he will drive anyway, without insurance, you need to consider whether or not you are ready to take that risk. You also should find out what your legal responsibility would be in the case of an accident. Could you be sued?

Your teen needs to know that so long as he lives in *your* home he will not drink and drive. And if he does, his privileges as a member of the family will be cut off, the last of which is the right to live there. Are you ready to enforce this through the legal authorities if necessary? Are you ready to deny him use of the furniture in his room by moving it out? Are you ready to withhold food or money to buy it? Would you withdraw laundry privileges? Are you ready to pack up every article of clothing that you have provided for him and lock it up? When all else fails, are you willing to let him know that he may live somewhere else until he is ready to follow the house rules, which *you* set? Are you willing to follow through by locking him out of the house? Are you willing to call the police if he then becomes angry and destructive and tries to break into the house? Are you willing to legitimize your threats by signing a complaint against your teenager, thereby admitting your inability to handle him and asking the juvenile court to intercede?

You are not a god and you cannot change your teen's behavior by direct intervention. But you can preserve your own dignity and property rights. By doing this you create the best atmosphere for change in him.

Blaming Keeps People Helpless

I will not spend a great deal of time on "blame," because its dynamics with the teen are the same as they are with the adult. Blame is what keeps the alcoholic merry-go-round going. The cast of characters with the teen drinker is the same as it is with the adult: the Enabler, the Provoker, and the Victim. The Yorks use slightly different labels: Rescuer, Persecutor, and Victim.

The teen alcohol user is great at playing the role of Victim, denying that he did anything that deserved getting a ticket, getting his license suspended, or being thrown into jail. When a parent refuses to clean up his mess for him, the teen may take the role of Provoker or Persecutor and blame the parent for all of his woe. He tells his parents that *they* were responsible for his unhappy life to begin with and now they are perpetuating his misery by not bailing him out of trouble.

The parents now play both Victims and Enablers. In order not to suffer further victimization and blame they bail him out—they rescue the wayward teen and unwittingly enable him to continue on with his drinking. They are teaching him a practical way of coping. The next time he gets in trouble he will again take the role of Victim, and if his parents don't help him, he will then assume the role of Provoker or Persecutor and blame them for his misery. And the outcome will probably be that they will once more rescue him and enable him to go around yet one more time on the merry-go-round.

Behavior Affects Parents and Kids

It is readily accepted in our society that parents' behavior and attitudes affect their children. In fact, it is carried to the ridiculous extreme that says the children would be obedient, well-mannered, responsible people if it were not for parents who are making them the way they are. But if the parents are "guilty," it is usually because of sins of omission rather than commission. The parents are sitting by help-lessly, accepting the misbehavior of the teens, and taking all the blame for it.

A teen's behavior affects parents too, a reality that reminds me of a sign I once saw: "Insanity is inherited—parents get it from their teenagers." Parents need to learn to react constructively to their teen's behavior. The Yorks say,

> What we have learned is that *first*, parents need help in reducing their anxiety about their children. Looking back, what we needed at this time was a third party who would intervene and tell us that we didn't have to accept our daughter's friends on their terms, and who would help us tell our daughters that they had to respect our values by not bringing raunchy people into our home.
>
> Just giving advice isn't enough. Parents need *active* support in dealing with the problem before they can get around to changing husband-wife dynamics. The tactic works much more effectively than that of merely asking parents to change something about themselves and then hoping the kids will change.[4]

Some of the best help for parents in this situation can come from a professional counselor who lets the parents know that they do not have to put up with the teen's drinking or other misconduct, and who is willing to tell the teen the same thing. Counselors must learn that teens need less "understanding" and more definition of their limits.

Taking a Stand

Setting limits requires that parents take a stand. The kids don't need to be understood or psychologized as much as they need to know that their parents have set boundaries on their behavior and that they intend to defend those boundaries.

Of course, taking a stand usually precipitates a crisis. It is at this moment that the parent stands on the brink of either a solution or another failure. A solution is in the offing when the parent stands

---

4. Ibid., p. 83.

firm, for as we shall see, out of a controlled crisis comes positive change.

On the other hand, parents who scream, cry, and yell—but ultimately back down—do the same thing that I described in the last chapter, where the Provoker adapts to the situation. Rather than face the crisis and take a stand, the parents adapt to a new set of rules or a new situation that they said they would never accept. Though this relieves the tension momentarily, it begins a new destructive turn of the merry-go-round. The teen is taught that the best way to deal with the parents' stand is to create a scene when a crisis looms, and the parents will back down and accept a new promise, a new set of rules, or a new arrangement—all of which last only until the next crisis.

One mistake a lot of parents make in taking a stand is that they take a position that is so momentous they do not have the courage to stand by it when the next crisis comes. For example, a parent may say, "I will not have a drunken child living in my house." But what happens when your son or daughter pounds on the door in the wee hours of the morning, too drunk to get the key in the lock? Do you stand firm and tell the teen to come back when he's sober and call the police if he becomes violent? If you are not ready to do that, you can refuse to grant the use of your car for a period of time. In any event, there is a line you can and should draw—and stand by that position. By doing so you will permit the crisis to open the door to a creative solution.

Controlled Crisis

Fear of consequences, more than anything else, keeps parents from permitting their teens to face the consequences of their behavior. By permitting a son or daughter to come home drunk again and again, parents try to relieve themselves of the anxiety of not knowing what may be happening to the errant teen. "Perhaps there has been an accident," the parent thinks—and then worries until the teen comes home.

It is this fear of consequences that both adult and teen drinkers use on their loved ones. They are confident that because of this fear the spouse or parent will always be there. If parents will let their children face the crisis without bailing them out, they will create more responsible children who realize that unless they exercise good judgment and control they themselves will suffer the consequences.

Parents should first take a stand that they can live with, small as it may be. You may decide to do something as simple as not giving your teen any more money. This may not keep him from drinking, but it will be the first small step in *your* change of behavior. When you successfully take this stand and discover that your teen accepts it, you will be ready to take the next stand.

What you are doing is reversing the process that your teen has employed on you. The errant adolescent first creates a crisis and gets you to adapt to it. He then creates a series of other crises, cleverly timed to get you to slowly but surely accept his behavior. If you do not adapt, he is always able to make *you* more afraid of the consequences than he is. Now is the time, even though you might be fainthearted, to let him know that you no longer are afraid of him or the consequences of his misconduct. He must begin to adapt to the new you.

Once you discover that he adapts to your not giving him any more handouts, you then can restrict the use of the car. How do you do that? You tell him he will not use it! If he has a key and says he will use it anyway, you tell him that if he does you will call the police and let them know that your car has been taken and is being used without your authorization. And you can also tell the authorities that you believe the driver may be drinking. *That* should get some action. But you better be ready to make a stand. Don't say you're going to do it and then back down when the occasion arises. You will then once again be an Enabler—*you* will be the adapter, not the teen. At least you can console yourself with the thought that it is better to face the crisis at the police station than at the morgue.

Community Support

You will find, however, that your task will be easier with the support of others. This is the ninth of the TOUGHLOVE beliefs. We hear about peer pressure again and again in connection with drinking and other irresponsible teenage behavior. Not only do teens feel pressure to go along with the crowd; the parents feel the pressure as well. "Everyone is doing it," they are told. Parents feel very alone in their attempt to control their teens. Adolescents have their support group that encourages them and forces the parents to adapt and accept their irresponsible behavior. Most parents have no such support group.

A new day has dawned! Parents are now discovering "parent pressure," which is an essential ingredient of TOUGHLOVE. Because parents are banding together to support each other emotionally and practically, they are finding out that every teen is *not* drinking and behaving irresponsibly.

The essence of the TOUGHLOVE support idea is to have weekly meetings for parents in which they receive the moral support of others who are going through the same problems. The support group also helps individual parents decide specifically where they are going to take their stand and when. For example, not giving a teen any money may seem like an ineffectual stand in a particular case, but it's a beginning. When this is carried off successfully, the parent is ready for the next stand and the next.

When it finally comes to denying the teen the right to come home, other parents in TOUGHLOVE will be available to provide food and shelter for the rebel and will act as intermediaries. This gives the parent moral support, and it makes the teen feel the pressure. Parental pressure will always win out if intelligently and consistently applied, simply because parents and teens are not equal legally and economically.

I urge parents who read this to join their local TOUGHLOVE group. If you don't know where to find such a group, if you are interested in starting one, write to:

> TOUGHLOVE
> Community Service Foundation
> P. O. Box 70
> Sellersville, PA 18960

Cooperation

The tenth TOUGHLOVE principle is that the essence of family life is cooperation, not togetherness:

> Cooperation values people working together and is people-centered. Togetherness keeps children immature and is child-centered.

Cooperation accepts the leadership of parents and the structure of family hierarchy. Togetherness requires no more of the child than merely being there.

Cooperation considers the good of the whole family, parents included. Togetherness accepts irresponsible and destructive teen behavior, which makes the family suffer.

Cooperation refuses to accept exploitation. Togetherness permits it.

The Yorks put it this way:

> The way you get cooperation from unruly young people is to withdraw the family resources which allow them to exploit their parents. By our insisting that they recognize their obligations to the family and its needs as a whole unit, young people will practice mutuality. We must value ourselves as much as we value our children.[5]

Cooperation demands mutual respect and will not fall prey to a twisted idea of love that is mere sentimentality—baby books and picture albums, memories of things that were and are no more. It is based not on feeling "loved" but on a mutual sense of responsibility that comes out of commitment to the good of others.

Love committed to the welfare of others is the highest and holiest form of love. It is easy to love when the loved one is lovable. But "tough love" requires that you care enough about a spouse or teen to be part of the destructive process no longer—a process that eventually winds up in a tragedy of far greater magnitude than if you took a stand.

Refusing to be part of the destructive process involves two things. First of all, if you have a spouse or a teenager at home who drinks too much, and *you* use alcohol at all, Christian liberty teaches that *you* have a responsibility to abstain. Liberty as taught in 1 Corinthians 8–11 asks even the moderate drinker to give up drinking if it is a cause of stumbling for someone else.

---

5. Ibid., p. 114.

In the second place, you must ask yourself if you are unwittingly contributing to the problem by allowing yourself to be an Enabler. Most people do not understand how they are contributing to a loved one's problem. Seriously consider the possibility that you are contributing to the problem and that you also need to change your ways.

Perhaps you have been praying for an answer to the heartache you have been experiencing with the alcoholic or problem drinker in your family. And perhaps you despair that your prayers will ever be answered. Could it be that you have been praying for the wrong thing? Could it be that you have been praying for change in the drinker and have failed to realize that the change must first begin in *you*?

> We, ignorant of ourselves,
> Beg often our own harms, which the wise powers
> Deny us for our good; so find we profit
> By losing of our prayers.
>
> *William Shakespeare*
> *Antony and Cleopatra*

Appendix A

A Chart of Alcohol Addiction and Recovery

A Chart of Alcohol Addiction and Recovery

To be read from left to right

occasional relief drinking

constant relief drinking commences

increase in alcohol tolerance

onset of memory blackouts

surreptitious drinking

increasing dependence on alcohol

urgency of first drinks

feelings of guilt

unable to discuss problem

memory blackouts increase

decrease of ability to stop drinking when others do so

crucial phase

drinking bolstered with excuses

grandiose and aggressive behavior

persistent remorse

efforts to control fail repeatedly

promises and resolutions fail

tries geographical escapes

loss of other interests

family and friends avoided

work and money troubles

unreasonable resentments

neglect of food

loss of ordinary will power

tremors and early morning drinks

decrease in alcohol tolerance

physical deterioration

onset of lengthy intoxications

cronic phase

moral deterioration

impaired thinking

drinking with inferiors

indefinable fears

unable to initiate action

obsession with drinking

vague spiritual desires

all alibis exhausted

complete defeat admitted

obsessive drinking continues in vicious circles

Reprinted from "Group therapy in Alcoholism," M. M. Glatt, M.D., D.P.M., Warlingham Park Hospital, in *The British Journal of Addiction,* Vol. 54, No. 2. This chart may be obtained from National Council on Alcoholism.

rehabilitation

enlightened and interesting way of life
opens up with road ahead to higher
levels than ever before

group therapy and mutual help continue

increasing tolerance

rationalizations recognized

contentment in sobriety

care of personal appearance

confidence of employer

first steps towards economic stability

increase of emotional control

appreciation of
real values

facts faced with courage

re-birth of
ideals

new circle of stable friends

new interests
develop

family and friends
appreciate efforts

adjustment to
family needs

natural rest and sleep

desire to escape goes

realistic thinking

return of self esteem

regular nourishment taken

diminishing fears of the
unknown future

appreciation of possibilities
of new way of life

start of group therapy

onset of new hope

physical overhaul by doctor

spiritual needs examined

assisted in making
personal stocktaking

right thinking begins

stops taking alcohol

meets former addicts normal and happy

learns alcoholism
is an illness

told addiction can be arrested

honest desire for help

Appendix B

The Average Effects
of Alcohol

The Average Effects of Alcohol

Bottles of Beer or Cocktails	Blood-Alcohol Level
1–2 • flushing of the skin • inhibitions begin to recede • heart speeds up • gaity	<u>4</u> 100's of 1%
3–4 • judgment is slower • giddiness • coordination is a bit off . . .	<u>6</u> 100's of 1%
5–6 • vision a bit blurred • speech a little fuzzy • reaction time slowed	<u>10</u> 100's of 1%
6–8 • staggering • seeing double • loss of balance	<u>16</u> 100's of 1%
15–20 • skin is clammy • pupils are dilated • unconsciousness	<u>40</u> 100's of 1%
20–25 • alcoholic poisoning = death	<u>50</u> 100's of 1%

The American Business Men's Research Foundation

Appendix C

Resources

Pamphlets and Other Resources

Alcoholics Anonymous, P. O. Box 182, Madison Square Station, New York, NY 10159 (for pamphlets on AA, Al-Anon, and Alateen).

American Council on Marijuana, 767 Fifth Avenue, New York, NY 10022.

Citizens for Informed Choices on Marijuana, 300 Broad St., Stanford, CT 06901.

Committees of Correspondence, Box 1590, Cathedral Station, New York, NY 10025.

CompCare Publications, 2415 Annapolis Lane, Minneapolis, MN 55441.

Drug Enforcement Administration: Prevention Program Section, Washington, DC 20537.

Families in Action, P. O. Box 15053, Atlanta, GA 30333.

Focus on the Family and Chemical Dependency, The US Journal of Drug and Alcohol Dependence, Inc., 2119-A Hollywood Blvd., Hollywood, FL 33020.

130

Interstate Movement Against Dangerous Drugs, P. O. Box 6272, Silver
   Spring, MD 20906.

National Drug Abuse Foundation, 6500 Randall Place, Falls Church, VA
   22044.

National Federation of Parents for Drug-Free Youth, P. O. Box 57217,
   Pennsylvania Avenue, Washington, D.C. 20037.

National Institute On Drug Abuse, P.O. Box 2305, Rockville, MD 20852.

Parent Resources and Information on Drug Education, Georgia State
   University, University Plaza, Atlanta, GA 30303.

Straight Talk, c/o Drug Fair Inc., 6295 Edsall Rd., Alexandria, VA 22314.

Residential Rehabilitation Programs

*Treatment facilities are found throughout the country. These organizations will
help locate the facility near you.*

Phoenix House Foundation, Inc., 164 West 74th Street, New York, NY
10023.
STRAIGHT, 3001 Gandy Boulevard, St. Petersburg, FL 33702.
Teen Challenge, 1445 Boonville Ave., Springfield, MO 65802.

Note: These resources are offered for reader information and are not
necessarily endorsed by the author or publisher of this book.

Bibliography

Books

Adkins, Jan. *The Craft of Making Wine*. New York: Walker Publishing, 1971.

Bengel, John Albert. *Gnomon of the New Testament*. Vol. 4. Edinburgh: T. & T. Clark, 1860.

Burgess, Louise Bailey. *Alcohol and Your Health*. Los Angeles: Charles Publishing, 1973.

Delitzsch, Franz. *Biblical Commentary on the Prophecies of Isaiah*. 2 vols. Grand Rapids: Wm. B. Eerdmans Publishing, 1954.

Delitzsch, Franz. *Biblical Commentary on the Proverbs of Solomon*. 2 vols. Grand Rapids: Wm. B. Eerdmans Publishing, n.d.

Edersheim, Alfred. *The Life and Times of Jesus the Messiah*. 2 vols. Grand Rapids: Wm. B. Eerdmans Publishing, 1950.

Fausset, The Rev. A. R. *A Commentary, Critical, Experimental, and Practical, of the Old and New Testaments*. Vol. 3, Job–Isaiah. Philadelphia: J. B. Lippincott, 1866.

Feyerabend, Prof. Karl. *Langenscheidt's Hebrew-English Dictionary to the Old Testament*. London: Methuen & Co., Ltd., 1956.

Hastings, James, (ed.). *A Dictionary of Christ and the Gospels*. New York: Charles Scribner's Sons, 1906.

Holden, C. *The Christian Book of Mystical Verse*, ed. A. W. Tozer, Harrisburg: Christian Publications, 1963.

Lenski, R. C. H. *The Interpretation of The Acts of the Apostles.* Minneapolis: Augsburg Publishing House, 1962.

Lightfoot, J. B. *Saint Paul's Epistles to the Colossians and to Philemon.* Grand Rapids: Zondervan Publishing House, 1897.

Milam, Dr. James R., and Katherine Ketcham. *Under the Influence.* New York: Bantam Books, 1983.

Peck, Harry Thurston (ed.). *Harper's Dictionary of Classical Literature and Antiquities.* New York: Cooper Square Publishers, 1962.

Smith, David. *The Days of His Flesh.* New York: Hodder and Stoughton, n.d.

Teachout, Robert P. *Wine The Biblical Imperative: Total Abstinence.* Columbia, S.C.: Richbarry Press, 1983.

Tregelles, Samuel Prideaux. *Gesenius' Hebrew and Chaldee Lexicon to the Old Testament Scriptures.* Grand Rapids: Wm. B. Eerdmans Publishing, 1857.

Van Impe, Dr. Jack, with Roger F. Campbell. *Alcohol: The Beloved Enemy.* Nashville: Thomas Nelson Publishers, 1980.

Wilbraham, Antony, and Michael Matta. *Introduction To Organic and Biological Chemistry.* 3d ed. (Menlo Park, Calif.: Benjamin Cummings Publishing, 1984.

Wilkerson, David. *Sipping Saints.* Old Tappan, N.J.: Fleming H. Revell, 1978.

York, Phyllis and David, and Ted Wachtel. *Toughlove.* New York: Bantam Books, 1983.

Younger, William. *Gods, Men, and Wine.* Cleveland: The Wine and Food Society Limited in Association with World Publishing Company, 1966.

Magazines

Christianity Today. Carol Stream, Ill.: Kenneth W. Johnson, Publisher.

Psychology Today. Washington, D.C.: Joseph Benjamin, Publisher.

Pamphlets Published by Al-Anon Family Group Headquarters, New York

"Al-Anon: Is It for You?"

"Alcoholism: A Merry-Go-Round Named Denial."

"Detachment."

"A Guide for the Family of the Alcoholic."

"My Wife Drinks Too Much."

Dissertation

Teachout, Robert P. "The Use of 'Wine,' in the Old Testament." Th.D. diss., Dallas Theological Seminary, Dallas, Texas, 1982.